PLAYING SMART

A Parent's Guide to Enriching, Offbeat Learning Activities for Ages 4-14

SUSAN K. PERRY

Edited by Pamela Espeland

Illustrated by L.T. Anderson

Free Spirit®
PUBLISHING

Library of Congress Cataloging-in-Publication Data
Perry, Susan K., 1946-
      Playing smart : a parent's guide to enriching, offbeat learning activities for ages 4 to 14 / Susan K. Perry.
          p. cm.
      Includes bibliographical references and index.
      ISBN 0-915793-22-9 :
      1. Family recreation. 2. Creative activities and seat work.
3. Creative thinking. I. Title.
      GV182.8.P38 1990
      790.1'91—dc20   90-40224
                                                                                                 CIP

10 9 8 7 6 5 4 3 2 1

Printed in the United States of America

Cover and book design by MacLean and Tuminelly

Free Spirit Publishing Inc.
400 First Avenue North, Suite 616
Minneapolis, MN 55401
(612) 338-2068

The following chapters have been adapted and greatly expanded from articles which first appeared in *Gifted Children Newsletter* (later renamed *Gifted Children Monthly*):

Chapter 2, original title "The Diary: Odyssey for Self-Exploration" © *GCN*, Feb. 1984, Vol. 5, No. 2

Chapter 4, original title "Find Adventure in Ordinary Places" © *GCN*, Dec. 1980, Vol. 1, No. 10

Chapter 5, original title "Cemetery: Learning Comes Alive for Gifted" © *GCN*, Oct. 1982, Vol. 3, No. 10

Chapter 6, original title "Photography: More Than Meets the Eye" © *GCN*, Mar. 1981, Vol. 2, No. 2

Chapter 8, original title "Gardening: Art and Science" © *GCM*, Mar. 1985, Vol. 6, No. 3

These materials have been used by permission of the publisher.

For Simon and Kevin,
my creative kids

"The quality of a life is determined by its activities."
— *Aristotle*

ACKNOWLEDGMENT

First and last, thanks to my husband, Stephen Perry, for introducing me to deeper levels of creativity, for taking me seriously (sometimes), and for putting aside his poetry (briefly) to assist me editorially.

CONTENTS

About the Author viii

Introduction ix
    The Latest Lore on Intelligence and Creativity ix
    Tips for Better Brainstorming..x
    How To Use This Book xi

Chapter 1: Instant Fun 1
    Waiting Games 1
    On the Road Again 7
    Paper-and-Pencil Quickies..9
    Using Common Senses 11
    RESOURCES 13

Chapter 2: Journal Journeys..................................15
    Nine Good Reasons for Your Child To Keep a Diary 16
    Getting Started 17
    Six Kinds of Diaries To Try 17
    Diary Rules...26
    RESOURCES 27

Chapter 3: Don't Read This Chapter! 31
    Paradoxes for Kids..31
    Tough Questions, Alibis, and More Mind Stretchers 35
    Change It, Finish It, Make It Up 39
    Book-Inspired Brain-Benders...42
    Imagination Towers 45
    RESOURCES 46

Chapter 4: Find Adventure in Ordinary Places.................49
    Where To Go and What To Do There 50
    Take In the Trash 53
    RESOURCES 54

Chapter 5: Learning Comes Alive at the Cemetery............55
    Preparing for Your Visit 55
    What To Look For: Names and Dates 56

What To Look For: Relationships 58

What To Look For: Beliefs 59

Digging Deeper: Related Investigations.....................60

RESOURCES 63

Chapter 6: Photography: More Than Meets the Eye..........65

Equipping the Young Shutterbug.........................66

Getting Started 67

Mastering the Medium...................................70

Picture This: Projects To Try 71

What To Do with All Those Photos:
Creative Possibilities...................................77

Photographic Side-Trips 78

New Uses for Old Photos...................................79

Photos that Move: Video Camera Fun...................................80

RESOURCES 81

**Chapter 7: Use Your Head:
Physical Activities that Exercise the Mind 83**

New Games 84

Creative Game-Changing...................................86

Body-Brain Workouts 90

Ten Ways To Make Walking Interesting Again 94

Sports Science 95

RESOURCES 97

**Chapter 8: Dirt, Worms, Bugs, and Mud:
Kids in the Garden 101**

Choosing Where and What To Plant....................102

Advance Planning...................................104

Learning in the Garden...................................106

Experiments for Budding Gardeners.....................110

Gardening and Aesthetics 113

RESOURCES 117

**Chapter 9: Mind Snacks:
Recipes for Kitchen Learning 121**

Getting Started 122

Over-the-Counter Learning 124

Food Trips: Going Beyond the Kitchen 127

Food Science 131

RESOURCES 133

Chapter 10: Cultural Diversity: It's All Relative..............**137**

From Tacos to Togas: Learning About Basic Needs 138

Exploring Cultural Attitudes..................................139

Nodding, Nose-Tapping, and More Body Language.........142

Time Traveling...144

Learning About the Arts 146

When Hello Means Good-bye:
Learning About Language.......................................148

Gods and Gardens: Comparative Mythology...................150

Twelve More Ways To Appreciate Cultural Diversity 152

Holidays Around the World.....................................155

Global Game-Playing...157

RESOURCES 160

Chapter 11: The Junior Psychologist...........................**167**

Dreamwork 167

Physiological Psychology: Exploring the Senses.............172

Memory Mysteries 176

Psychology Pursuits...179

RESOURCES 183

**SPECIAL SECTION: Introducing Famous
Authors Through Their Books for Children**.....................**187**

Children's Books by Famous Authors:
Recommended Readings..189

Selected List of Publishers **201**

Index **205**

ABOUT THE AUTHOR

Susan K. Perry is an independent writer with more than 450 articles in national and regional publications, including *Seventeen, Woman's World, USA Today,* and the *Los Angeles Times.* Her specialties are family and educational topics, and she is Contributing Editor of *L.A. Parent Magazine.* She won a First Place Award of Excellence in the Parenting Publications of America 1989 Annual Competition, judged by the Medill School of Journalism at Northwestern University.

Perry obtained a Master's Degree in The Administration of Human Development Programs from Pacific Oaks College in 1978, a degree which emphasizes how children and adults learn. She founded and directed an unusual and successful early childhood program called Discovery House School. She was a teacher for the Gifted Children's Association of Los Angeles, for which she developed innovative courses in human relations, creativity, science, and reading.

She is the mother of two teenage sons and lives in Los Angeles with her husband, poet Stephen Perry.

Introduction

Children, especially bright ones, need enrichment at home. And children of all ages love attention, especially from you. *Playing Smart* offers hundreds of unusual ways for kids and parents to spend time together. It's about the fun people can have while learning, and the learning that goes on while having fun.

It's *not* about glitter and eggshells, or more of the same contrived activities kids already do at school. Nor is it about getting your child to read more, write better, or score higher in math and science. But children who experiment with the activities described here will find their reading, writing, calculating, and thinking skills enhanced as a natural by-product of their explorations.

Using this book as a guide, you and your child will survey new subjects ranging from cultural relativity to photography, journal keeping, psychology, and the mental side of physical education. You'll learn how to learn wherever you are: at the doctor's office, in the kitchen, in the garden, in the car. You'll go places you may not have thought of before, including the cemetery.

The activities in *Playing Smart* stress creative thinking. Most of them don't require complicated preparations or equipment; you and your child can do them in small bits of time on ordinary days, without making a big deal about it. Many involve nothing more than mental interactions between parent and child. All of them are meant to feel like *play*. Kids do enough work at school. The time you spend together should be time you enjoy.

THE LATEST LORE ON INTELLIGENCE AND CREATIVITY

Since many parents hope to nourish intelligence and creativity in their children, research is constantly underway to figure out what it takes. Here's a smattering of conclusions and recommendations from recent studies:

▶ Creativity — the ability to produce novel ideas — thrives when children are allowed to be spontaneous, messy, and silly. Kids are most creative when they feel free to be playful.

▶ Praise your child's efforts and ideas, especially the offbeat ones. But don't evaluate or offer rewards for creative work.

▶ To encourage creative thinking, take seriously your child's unconventional responses. Try never to respond with creativity stiflers like, "That wouldn't work," or "That doesn't make any sense!"

▶ Spend time simply *talking* to your child about ideas. A survey of highly successful adults found that their parents had often done this with them.

▶ Share your enthusiasms with your child, and expose her to as many different interests and fields as you can. But don't insist or urge too strongly a child who clearly isn't interested. Better yet, follow your child's lead and share her enthusiasms.

TIPS FOR BETTER BRAINSTORMING

A number of the activities in *Playing Smart* suggest brainstorming. The purpose of brainstorming is to free the mind to think up as many answers to a question, or solutions to a problem, as possible.

Brainstorming isn't appropriate for closed-ended problems that have a single correct solution, such as, "What's the capital of California?" But it's wonderful for questions like, "Name all the ways you can think of to get your teacher's attention." The most creative thinkers are those who come up with the most responses: Throw something. Shout. Tap her on the shoulder. Break a window. Pass a note. Pretend to be sick. Bang on your desk. Sing. Pop a balloon. Play an instrument. Wink at her. Steal her chalk. And so on.

Brainstorming is a skill that can be taught, practiced, and developed. The more your child uses this skill, the more creative a thinker he will be. Here are some tips for helping your child to be a better brainstormer:

▶ When you present a question or a problem, encourage your child to give any and every response that comes to mind. There are no "right" or "wrong" responses.

▶ All of us have resident "internal critics" — voices inside our minds that say, "But that's too silly, too impractical, too expensive, too bizarre…" Tell your child that brainstorming is a time when that voice should shut up! If your child has a habit of negative self-talk, this is your chance to do something about it.

▶ Brainstorming tends to generate a lot of ideas. Naturally, some are better than others. But the purpose of brainstorming isn't to judge or eliminate ideas. The only time you should select some ideas and not others is when there's a compelling reason to do this — and when all possible ideas have been brought out into the open.

HOW TO USE THIS BOOK

I have not assigned recommended ages to the activities in *Playing Smart*. Most are adaptable for any age, right through adult. A good approach is to read the introductory material in each chapter, then skim the activities to become familiar with the ideas presented. Then, at dinner, after breakfast on weekends, at bedtime, or whenever, flip open the book to whatever looks like fun, and suggest an activity or bring up an idea to talk about.

When you introduce new concepts to a child at the lower end of the four-to-fourteen range, simplify the language as much as you need to. The same imagination sparker will bring about entirely different results when used again a year or two later. If your child is older, say eight or nine and up, you'll find a bonanza of advanced activities that assume you have been raising a curious, creative, independent thinker all along.

Are some activities more suited to boys than girls, and vice versa? Not at all. The reason I mix "hes," "shes," and "theys" in random order throughout this book is simple: Since girls are half the world, they deserve half the pronouns. If you have a girl child, you shouldn't have to read "he…" over and over, yet one becomes tired of reading (and writing) "he or she" and "your children...they..." So I compromised. You know best what your child is like. If a particular activity looks like it fits, try it.

What if your child becomes bored with an activity, or would rather do something else? Let go! There's nothing more deadening to a child's interest than insisting on continuing or completing some activity because it's supposed to be fun.

Finally, each chapter ends with a list of resources — books, games, and more — should you want to pursue a topic or interest area further. Some are for children, some are for adults, some are for either or both. I've recommended some age levels, but you're the one who knows the most about your child's reading ability and attention span. Many children will gladly look through books far above their reading level, if they're interested in what the books are about.

Not all of the books I've mentioned will be available at your library. The ones from major publishers are easy to order through most bookstores. To help you locate the many smaller or independent publishers whose books might not be found in stores, I've included a Selected List of Publishers, with addresses, on pages 201-203.

Now, begin playing smart...

Susan K. Perry
August 1990

CHAPTER 1

Instant Fun

The year my son Kevin was eight, one of our car pool drivers was often delayed picking the kids up from school. One afternoon, when Kevin was dropped off at home particularly late, I asked him what had happened. He said that school personnel had told him to wait for his ride in the room next to the principal's office. Hadn't he been awfully bored for that half hour? "No," he said, "I kept busy finding the pictures in the wallpaper."

That's what "instant fun" is all about: keeping creatively occupied when a wait is unavoidable. Here's a multitude of ideas you and your child can use when the doctor or dentist makes you wait, when a car trip seems endless, or whenever you have minutes to spare. For many of these activities, a group can play as well as two.

WAITING GAMES

▶ Make up stories about the people around you. You can either take turns — one sentence or idea each — or just

improvise together and see where the story goes and who wants to contribute the next bit of information or plot turn.

Example: Let's say there's a man with a briefcase seated across the room. Perhaps he's a spy or a counter-spy. Perhaps he's on his way to deliver the secret of how to make a new type of weapon, one which causes people's shoes to become untied so that they trip on them. Perhaps he's a movie star traveling in disguise.

▶ One of you chooses a person or an object (a sofa, a cluttered desk) and both of you look hard at it for a short time. Then close your eyes or face in the other direction, and take turns telling everything you can remember about the chosen person or scene.

This is more than a memory game — it sharpens visual perception. You'll find yourselves improving with repeated play.

▶ Play a version of "I Spy." Think of something in the room, and have the other person guess what it is by asking five yes-or-no questions about it. Or think of something not in the room and allow ten or twenty questions.

Example: You're thinking of a frying pan. Your child asks questions like, "Is it bigger than a salt shaker?" "Is it hard?" "Is it in our house?" "Do I ever use it?" "Is there more than one?"

▶ Play "Opposites." You say a word, and your child comes up with an opposite.

Examples: Light, dark; happy, sad; angelic, devilish; compete, cooperate.

▶ Play "Connections" or "No-Connections." You say a word, and your child tries to think of a word that's related to it in some way, however far-fetched. Then she has to explain the relationship or connection.

Example: If you say "mind," she might say "walk," explaining that you use your mind to command your legs to walk.

For a more complex version, your child says a word, such as "book." Then you name a word that seems to be completely unrelated, such as "squirrel." Her task is to make a connection. For instance: When you cut down trees to make paper to make books, squirrels are left homeless.

▶ Make up New Year's Resolutions for famous people or animals.

Examples: A porcupine might resolve to "stick to it from now on." A penguin might decide to "dress casually." Pee Wee Herman could pledge to start a weight-lifting program.

▶ Play "I Packed My Grandmother's Trunk." The first person says, "I packed my grandmother's trunk, and in it I put an artichoke" (or anything else starting with A). Each person then adds something new and creative to the line-up, in alphabetical order. The hard part is repeating everything that has been said before.

Example: "I packed my grandmother's trunk, and in it I put an artichoke, a bomb, a canary, and a daisy...."

▶ While stuck waiting in line, closely investigate the passing people parade for individual details.

Examples: What is each person's most outstanding quality? One may be dressed fashionably, another may look unusually happy.

Or assess trends: Do most of the young men have short hair? Are most of the young women wearing dangly earrings? How many females are carrying handbags? What about the males? How many people are wearing glasses?

▶ Play "Firsts and Lasts." Choose a category, such as geography, people, animals, foods, or plants. (With an older child, you can choose a more limited, challenging category.) One of you names an item in the category, and the other names an item that begins with the last letter of the item named by the previous player.

Example: If the category is "animals" and you say "dog," your child might respond with "goat." "Turkey" might be next.

▶ If you know a foreign language, or even a little bit of one, teach your child a couple of words while you wait.

▶ Look around, pick out a common object, and invent new ways to use it. Then imagine it many times larger, or smaller, and think of more ways to use it. Could its parts be rearranged to multiply its uses? What might a visitor from another planet do with it?

▶ Make up your own Sniglets. Invented by comedian Rich Hall, Sniglets are defined as "any word that doesn't appear in the dictionary, but should."

Examples: From Hall's book, *Sniglets:* "Memnants: The chipped or broken m&m's at the bottom of the bag." "Conagraphs: The raised relief squares on an ice-cream cone."

▶ Take turns humming familiar songs and guessing the title of the other person's song.

▶ Make up a haiku about your surroundings or your mood. Haiku is a Japanese verse form of three unrhymed lines that add up to seventeen syllables, arranged 5-7-5. What counts in this case are originality and fun, not artistic durability!

Examples:

"Green-leafed plant in the
still air of a waiting room,
when is it my turn?"

"Waiting in the doc-
tor's office isn't fun, the
time goes so slowly."

▶ Take turns coming up with thought provokers like, "List ten ways to complete the statement, 'I am…,'" or "What would you do if you had only six months to live, or six months with no responsibilities at all?"

▶ Make up a perky advertising slogan for a dull product.
   Example: To sell plain white shoelaces: "If the shoe fits, it's laced by Ace."

▶ Ask your child to choose a year in your life (say, when you were five or ten years old). Then try to remember everything you can about that year, from who your friends were, to what you wore, to what your room looked like. Then choose a year in your child's life and see what he can remember about it. Add your memories to his for a more complete picture.

▶ Even if you have no paper or pencils with you, you can still play tic-tac-toe. Imagine the number pad on a touch-tone telephone, with 1-2-3 across the top row, 4-5-6 across the middle row, and 7-8-9 across the third row. Now take turns placing your X or 0 in one space at a time, naming that space by its number on the pad ("I put an X in 3," "I put an O in 6"). It takes a bit of concentration, but it works.

▶ Think of a variety of things you could never be or do: "I could never be a pirate." "I could never ride a dinosaur." "I could never write a book and build a house at the same time." "I could never fly." Then talk about how you could be or do those things in one way or another.
   Examples: "I could be a pirate in a play." "I could 'ride' a dinosaur skeleton in a museum." "I could hire someone to build the house and write a book about that." "I could fly in an airplane."

▶ Play "What's the Question?" Someone makes a one-sentence statement which answers an unknown question, and the other person tries to find a question that fits. Encourage creativity and humor.
   Examples: Answer: "Play marbles in the rain." Question: "What should a child made of sugar never do?" Answer: "Rusty screws." Question: "What did you eat for breakfast?" Answer: "A sheep with a wig." Question?

▶ Make a fist with your thumb inside. Use a pen to draw eyes, a nose, and hair on the outside of your forefinger. Move your thumb to turn your hand into a puppet. Or draw on your child's hand instead, or on both yours and his, so your two "hand puppets" can have a conversation.

▶ Together, design exercises you can do while you wait, wherever you are.

Examples: Show your child what isometrics are (tensing various parts of the body, holding them for a brief count, then relaxing them). Create an exercise for each part of the body, from wrists to toes. See if you can wiggle one eyebrow or one ear.

This activity is especially recommended for longer waits, when most children get squirmy or cranky.

■ ■ ■ ■ ■ ■ ■ ■ ■ ■ ■ ■ ■ ■ ■ ■ ■ ■ ■

HOW TO PACK AN EMERGENCY FUN BAG

Especially if your child is young, you should always carry an Emergency Fun Bag in your car. Then you can take it along on appointments that might otherwise leave you sitting toyless and bookless in a waiting room. Here are some things to put in your Emergency Fun Bag:

▶ a ball (either a tennis ball or a tiny rubber one)

▶ a small sewing kit

▶ paper, pencils, pens, and crayons

▶ finger puppets

▶ a deck of cards

▶ magnets

▶ a yo-yo

▶ a mirror (preferably metal and unbreakable)

▶ wax or clay for modeling

▶ miniature travel versions of popular games like Connect Four, Yahtzee, Othello, Mastermind, Memory, Battleship, Hi-Q, backgammon, chess, or checkers (available at specialty games stores, department stores, and toy stores)

Pack your "emergency fun" in a tote bag, a small nylon carry-on, even a lunchbox. You may want to leave it in the car between trips, to make sure you don't forget it at home.

■ ■ ■ ■ ■ ■ ■ ■ ■ ■ ■ ■ ■ ■ ■ ■ ■ ■ ■ ■

ON THE ROAD AGAIN

The automotively creative kid will be able to come up with lots of ways to keep busy while cruising the highways. Help out in duller moments with ideas like these:

▶ Look for distinguishing characteristics.

Examples: How many cars have whitewalls? Are most of the cars old or new? (In some states, you can tell relative age by the sequence of numbers on the license plates.) How many different car makes can you identify? How many things can you find wrong with the cars you see, such as wheel wobble, dented fenders, broken trunk locks, cracked windows, bent antennas?

▶ Play the oldest on-the-road game of all: Count things! The possibilities are endless, from the cars on passing trains to horses, barns, fire hydrants, or billboards. Narrow this down further to billboards with pictures of women, or of women selling cars. As you drive through towns or cities, count people with briefcases, people carrying paper sacks, women wearing blue skirts, and so on. Or count everything you pass that begins with a B.

▶ Notice unusual bumper-sticker slogans, then make up some of your own.

▶ Notice and count custom license plates. Come up with ideas for custom plates for people you know.
    Examples: NML-DR ("Animal Doctor") for a veterinarian, or DR-NML ("Doctor Enamel") for your dentist; 2X2R4 for a math teacher.

■ ■ ■ ■ ■ ■ ■ ■ ■ ■ ■ ■ ■ ■ ■ ■ ■ ■ ■ ■

FUN WITH TONGUE TWISTERS

Try saying these quickly, three times in a row:

1. Cows graze in groves on grass which grows in grooves in groves.

2. Six slippery seals slipping silently ashore.

3. Barbara burned the brown bread badly.

4. A regal rural ruler.

Make up your own tongue twisters. Take turns choosing a letter of the alphabet for the other person to work with. Or take turns coming up with hard-to-pronounce phrases for each letter of the alphabet, starting with A. Or begin with one-syllable words, then try to trip the tongue with words of two or more syllables.

Twisters that combine two or more sounds are super hard to say, as in "Shave a cedar shingle thin," or:

Theophilus Thistle, the thistle sifter,
sifted a sieve of unsifted thistle.
If Theophilus Thistle, the thistle sifter,
sifted a sieve of unsifted thistles,
where is the sieve of unsifted thistles Theophilus Thistle,
the thistle sifter, sifted?

PAPER-AND-PENCIL QUICKIES

▶ One of you draws a squiggle or part of a picture. Then alternate adding pieces to it. The final drawing will probably look entirely different from what the first drawer had in mind.

▶ Write a letter together. Both of you compose it; either one of you can write it. Your letter can be a suggestion or complaint directed to your local council person or the President of the United States, a friendly missive to a relative or pen pal, or anything else you choose.

▶ Teach your child to make lists. Brainstorm different kinds.
   Examples: A "Why Not?" list of things to do next summer, when your school-age child has more free time. "Why not milk a cow…." "Why not watch a sunset…." Other lists might include "Healthy Snack Foods To Stock Up On," "Friends To Invite To My Next Birthday Party," "Chores I Can Do To Earn Extra Money," and so on.

▶ Have your child begin a "Wish List" of things she'd like for her birthday or holidays. (Of course, let her know she won't necessarily get everything on the list, but that you'll pick and choose from it when you need inspiration.)
   A "Wish List" can go beyond the merely personal and greedy to include wishes for world peace, an end to hunger, and other altruistic hopes and dreams. Talk about what each of you could do to help make such fantasies come true.

▶ If you're secure enough, invite your child to write up a "report card" for you. (If you're lucky, you'll get an "A" for Effort.) Ask him to grade you on such abilities and achieve-

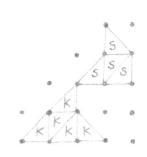

ments as Knowledge of Parenting, Learns from Mistakes, Generous with Allowance, Has Dinner Ready on Time, Helps with Homework, etc.

▶ Play dot-to-dot. Fill a few square inches with evenly spaced dots. You and your child take turns drawing a line connecting any two adjoining dots, either up and down or across. The object is to complete as many boxes as possible. Whenever a player completes a box, she gets to place her initials inside it and take another turn. When all the boxes are completed, the player with the most boxes wins.

For variety, play this with triangles. Begin by drawing a large un-outlined triangle filled with dots and proceed to take turns connecting lines to form small triangles.

▶ Make paper airplanes from sheets of paper. See whose flies the farthest.

▶ Play "Finger Pool." Fold a piece of paper into a compact chunk and take turns flicking your fingers at it to make it cross a table.

▶ Borrow from the game *Mad Libs* (see Resources, page 13) and make up silly sentences. One of you writes a sentence (keeping it secret), leaving one word out, then asks the other person for a word of the needed part of speech.

Example: Your sentence is, "The hungry _____ nibbled at the little boy's toe." You ask your child for a noun, or perhaps something as specific as an animal. He fills in the blank with "helicopter," "encyclopedia," "aardvark," or anything he chooses. Read your sentence aloud, including his word.

▶ Try your own homemade version of Droodles, a game introduced by Roger Price in his book, *Droodles* (see Resources, page 13). Draw something that looks like what you say it is, but only with a great stretch of the imagination.

Examples: A single straight line could be "what you see through a closed elevator door." Several straight lines could be "food's view of a fork."

USING COMMON SENSES

▶ With your finger, trace a design on your youngster's back. See if she can tell what you've drawn. Work your way up from letters of the alphabet to bananas, tables, chairs, and trees. "Draw" slowly. Take turns.

▶ Using a mirror, reverse the words on a menu or a magazine article. See if your child can read them backwards.

▶ Have your child close his eyes. Then pull something out of your purse, pocket, or briefcase and ask him to figure out what it is by touch. Can he distinguish a penny from a dime, a house key from a car key?

▶ Have your child close her eyes and imagine she's inside a spaceship, an Indian tepee, a castle, or a hot-dog factory. What does she see, hear, smell, taste, touch? This activity increases your child's ability to form mental images.

▶ Tune in to your senses. Be very quiet and see how many sounds you can hear. See if you can figure out what each individual sound is.

  Examples: At home, these may include the sound of the refrigerator's motor, somebody mowing a lawn, cars or trucks in the distance, birds chirping, people walking by, doors closing, and so on.

  Carry this further, and try to distinguish odors. Then guess textures.

  Examples: In a doctor's office, your child may feel the smoothness of a leather sofa, the woolliness of a carpet, the patchy roughness of a plastered wall, the veins of a plant's leaf, and so on.

▶ Take a walk together. Even in the city, this can be a nature walk.

  How many natural things can you notice? Trees, plants, weeds coming through cracks? What kinds of trees do you see? Do they all have different seed pods? Look for pigeons and sparrows in parks, on window ledges, on rooftops,

peeking from behind store signs, and nesting on top of office air conditioners.

Bring along some paper and a soft pencil or crayon to make tree bark rubbings. Hold the paper against the bark, then rub it with the pencil or crayon. The bark's pattern will be transferred to the paper.

■ ■

THE "WHAT IF" GAME

Explore hypothetical situations, brainstorming as many imaginative responses as possible. These can be personal, such as:

1. What if you had a million dollars? A hundred million dollars?

2. What if you could never leave your house again? What five objects, and what one person, would you choose to have there with you?

3. What if you could change your name — what would you choose?

4. What if you could choose to have another sense — something besides sight, hearing, touch, smell, and taste?

5. What if you could be reborn at another time, past or future? When would you choose, and why?

6. What if you could clone yourself?

These pretend situations can also go beyond the personal, as in:

1. What would happen if gravity were twice as strong? Half as strong?

2. What if nobody had to work for a living?

3. What if people could choose to change their sex easily, as often as they wanted to?

Make up your own "What Ifs" to explore and discuss.

■ ■

RESOURCES

The Big Book of Kids' Lists by Sandra Choron (World Almanac Publications, 1985). Over 250 lists of interest to youngsters on topics ranging from ice-cream flavors to movie monsters. Indexed.

Droodles by Roger Price (Price Stern Sloan, 1966). This little booklet contains dozens of simple, odd drawings with unexpected titles and explanations. Highly recommended to get creative juices flowing.

Funny Answers to Foolish Questions by Maureen Kushner (Sterling, 1988). Each foolish question — "Why does your room look like a tornado hit it?" — has several answers as silly as, "Because I had a brainstorm."

HearthSong, P.O. Box B, Sebastopol, California 95473-0601; toll-free telephone 1-800-325-2502. Request a catalog from this distributor of toys, books, games, and tools for imaginative play. You'll find colorful beeswax for modeling, "pocket pals" (tiny felt dolls that travel well), and hand-painted finger puppets.

The Kids' Book of Questions by Gregory Stock, Ph.D. (Workman, 1988). This thought-provoking book is a big hit with kids of all ages, who love reading and answering the questions that range from silly ("If you were offered $100 to kiss someone you liked in front of your school class, would you do it?") to serious ("When you make a mistake, do you make up excuses? If so, do you think people believe you?").

The Klutz Book of Card Games (for Card Sharks and Others) (Klutz Press, 1990) comes packaged with a deck of cards. It includes instructions for twenty popular card games and two card tricks, plus pointers on playing well. A good item for an Emergency Fun Bag.

Mad Libs (Price Stern Sloan, many editions). For ages 8 and up. This party game in the form of a book can be played by any number of people, anywhere, anytime. Each version is a tablet of stories with blank spaces where key words have been omitted. Without knowing the title or theme of the story, the reader asks players to come up with adjectives, nouns, verbs, or other parts of speech, as specified under each blank. After the blanks are filled in, the reader reads the silly story aloud.

Sniglets by Rich Hall (Collier Books, 1984). "Words that don't appear in the dictionary, but should."

World's Toughest Tongue Twisters by Joseph Rosenbloom (Sterling, 1987). For ages 7–10. Five hundred of the most difficult tanglers of tongues.

CHAPTER 2
Journal Journeys

The younger your children are when they embark on the adventure of self-exploration via journal keeping, the broader their long-term insights and benefits will be. Recently, when my oldest son re-read the four- and five-year-old entries in his first diary, he mourned that he hadn't begun when he was two or three!

With a preschooler, all you need to do is zero in on a moment of special happiness or sadness. You can say something like, "Let's write that feeling down; it'll make you feel better." The re-reading is its own reward for the child — and a new diarist will have been born.

Though a child can start a diary at any age and restart it in varying forms whenever interest is high, one particularly suitable time is during the turbulent preteen years. A personal journal can help fulfill the strong need for self-expression and privacy children experience at this stage.

NINE GOOD REASONS FOR YOUR CHILD TO KEEP A DIARY

Why should a growing person keep a written record of thoughts, feelings, and actions? Although there are many reasons, depending on the individual and on the type of diary chosen, the process of committing to paper a permanent history of daily life provides the following general benefits to almost any child:

1. catharsis, in having a safe place to express feelings

2. insight into growing up, and help in dealing with change

3. improved communications and trust between parent and child, and increased self-esteem (as long as parents never belittle anything their child writes, or invade their child's privacy without invitation)

4. better powers of observation and sharpened senses as the diarist turns not only inward to feelings, but outward to record actual happenings (one begins to notice much more — smells, colors, changing seasons)

5. capture of early memories before they fade

6. the development of a writing style (a diary is a good place to experiment freely, without having to pay attention to grammar or spelling)

7. improved language skills

8. a more active imagination, perhaps inspiring further nonfiction or fiction writing and other creative projects

9. pleasure in the act itself

Writing a diary can be an art form in its own right, providing pleasure in the writing and greater joy in simply living, since details are more deeply seen and felt when one is considering every experience as a potential diary entry.

GETTING STARTED

What to write in? Almost any notebook will do for a child's diary. Though tiny notebooks are cute and portable, a larger format encourages experimentation and ease. A medium-sized bound book with blank pages works best for many people. Your child can choose his own, or you can give him one as a gift. An attractive cover may be appreciated, and a lock can be reassuring.

Undated pages are best, because if the child skips dated pages he may feel he's "not doing it right," which can cause him to lose his motivation. The worst case is when a diarist feels he has to apologize to his own notebook for "not writing for so long." Many calendar diaries, especially the five-year kind with only a few lines allowed per day, don't allow enough space to be creative.

What to write with? Pencil smears, but some people demand erasability. Others like to use a variety of colored pens. If the aesthetics of crossing out aren't pleasing, you might offer your child correction fluid for errors.

What if your child is too young to write? You can spend five or ten minutes a day writing down exactly what he or she dictates. Allow complete freedom, even for entries that range from the mundane to the highly charged. Read back any and all entries as the child asks. A line or two a day is fine if you want to teach the value of daily journaling, but a voluble child may dictate pages at a time.

What if your child can't think of anything to write? Ask some leading questions: What's your best friend like, and why do you enjoy each other? How would you change your school?

Finally, consider keeping a diary yourself and sharing parts of it with your youngster.

SIX KINDS OF DIARIES TO TRY

Depending on your child's personality and special interests, you can lead her to begin a specific kind of journal, or a combination of several. Here are some possibilities to explore:

1. *The Personal Feelings Diary.* "I want to write, but more than that, I want to bring out all kinds of things that lie

buried deep in my heart," wrote Anne Frank in *The Diary of a Young Girl.*

In a personal feelings diary, intermittent entries are as appropriate as daily ones. Young children can dictate these diaries. When your child records and perhaps analyzes her emotions, she may feel calmer. When you keep a diary of your feelings, you're writing to your future self.

As a young teenager, I read and re-read my own diary entries almost daily. Such self-absorption is normal at that age, as is the teen's desire to gain perspective during a tumultuous period. When writer Gail Godwin re-reads old diaries, she jots down a word or two to her former self as a way of setting the record straight.

The youthful diaries of many famous people have been published, whether they planned it that way or not: Theodore Roosevelt, Louisa May Alcott, Karen Horney, and Margaret O'Brien are just a few examples that come to mind. (Of course, some people write with an eye to posterity.)

Some starting points for a feelings diary are:

▶ Record your emotions about some problem in your life.

▶ Try to imagine, in writing, what would happen if you made one decision as opposed to another.

▶ Write about your friends or parents and what they mean to you.

▶ Write about what makes you happy or sad.

At age 4 1/2, Simon was very feelings-oriented, as these entries illustrate:

I am a good boy. I played, that's all I did today. I went to the zoo with my school. I am mad at Lisa. And I am also mad at Markie because he hits me every time I go to school.

Even my teacher is dumb and no one can tell her that, because she didn't let me go up the stairs by myself today.

Now I have something to punch: my frog. In fact I love Mommy right now. There's nothing I like more than Mommy. I love my frog sometimes and sometimes I don't.

I am mad at Daddy and I am also mad at me because I didn't want to do such a bad thing and I don't know if I did [take his wrench].

Today I'm mad. Mommy went to the store but I wanted her to get a present for me, but I have too much toys and too much books.

2. ***The Dream Journal.*** The child dictates or writes down his dreams each morning while they're still vivid. Some tips for this type of journaling are:

▶ Your child should keep a pen and paper, or a tape recorder, within easy reach of his bed.

▶ Before your child goes to sleep, he needs to tell himself, "Tonight I will remember what I dream." (You can remind him to do this at first.)

▶ Some dream journalists set alarms to wake themselves up at odd hours, the better to interrupt dreams-in-progress. I think it's best for a child to wake up naturally and recall the last dream he had, which is the longest and most detailed.

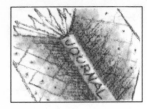

▶ The more details your child records, the better. He can include moods, colors, and any ideas about what the dream might refer to or mean.

At 5 1/2, Simon enjoyed sharing his dreams:

Hello. What I dreamed about was my girlfriend. My girlfriend was talking Martian talk. We were saying, "Poomp, doomp, dingerp." It was really a nice dream, very nice and sweet and lovable.

3. **The Activities Diary.** Ordinary-seeming "what-I-did-today" accounts may eventually lead to expression of feelings. But don't pressure the child who may find such articulation difficult.

Activities diaries are often kept every day, always with dated entries. Suggest that your child write at least three or four sentences daily.

Sometimes this kind of diary is kept for a certain length of time and is used to record a particular series of developments. For example, your child might keep a journal during a family vacation. Or she might record a new puppy's early growth and antics.

Kevin, 4 1/2, preferred an activities-based journal, shown by these typical entries:

We got a typewriter that's broken. I held the mouse at school and I put it back in the cage.

I rided my bike today. We went to a party and we got little hats.

Today we drove around and they wouldn't let people get in the snow unless they lived there. And we tried to go to Mt. Wilson but the road was blocked by a sign that said "Road Closed."

Kevin at age 5:

I went camping for four days. It was very fun. I saw a movie there. I had campfires there. I made some friends there. I saw a cave there. The ocean used to be over the whole mountain. I walked through a tree. We walked up a trail. It's going to start all over again: the ocean is going to go over the mountains again, in about a million years. We went on a long walk and I found a little daisy flower. I dug an ant hole. I climbed a high tree. I flew a play plane. I got it stuck in a tree lots of times.

4. **The Scrapbook Journal.** When presented with a blank book, some children, especially younger ones, feel more comfortable expressing themselves with drawings. Photographs can be used, too. In fact, a journal can be combined with a more inclusive album in which your child places a variety of small souvenirs: movie stubs, fortune-cookie slips, party invitations, proverbs, jokes, and so on.

■ ■ ■ ■ ■ ■ ■ ■ ■ ■ ■ ■ ■ ■ ■ ■ ■ ■ ■ ■

TIME IN A CAPSULE

A "time capsule," in which children capture an ordinary day, is a variation on the scrapbook journal. Help your child think in terms of seeking out everyday items guaranteed to bring back memories a year, five years, or twenty years from now. The time capsule's form can vary from a book to slips of paper tucked into a large envelope. Drawings or photographs may be added.

Here are some questions you can use to start your child thinking about this:

▶ What time do you get up? Go to bed? Do you read in bed at night? For how long?

▶ What are you reading today? What's your all-time favorite book?

▶ What do you eat on a typical day, including nibbles? Do you watch TV or read while you eat?

▶ How much TV do you watch each day? Do you have a favorite show? Is there one or more you hate? Is there a commercial you're learning to sing?

▶ What chores are you supposed to do around the house? Which ones do you do without being reminded?

▶ Did you buy a toy or a hobby or sports item today or recently?

▶ What was the last movie you saw? How much did it cost? Tell who starred in it and what happened.

> How much does gasoline cost in your neighborhood?

> How do you get to school?

> What do you do with your friends when they come over?

> How much is your allowance and what did you do with it this week? Are you saving up for something special?

> Did you argue with someone today? About what?

> What do you collect?

> What's your height today? Your weight?

Here are some items you might suggest your child include in a time capsule:

> the front page, some ads, and movie and TV listings from today's newspaper

> pictures or drawings of your bedroom, your school, your secret hide-out

> a gum wrapper, trading card, homework paper

Finally, encourage your child to:

> Write a message to yourself to be read a year from today, and perhaps another to be read a long time from now.

■ ■ ■ ■ ■ ■ ■ ■ ■ ■ ■ ■ ■ ■ ■ ■ ■ ■ ■ ■

5. *The Writer's Journal.* This type of journal, with its detailed observations, is particularly suitable for verbally capable children. A writer's journal may also include ideas, notes about projects, plans, feelings, overheard dialogue, poems, and so on. Some children enjoy writing lists, a broad category encompassing inventories of gripes, wishes, resolutions, even books read. These materials are then available to be reprocessed, if the child desires, into stories, poems, or other forms.

In the June 1982 issue of *The Writer,* author Mary Phraner Warren notes that instead of simply "Today I went to the dentist," a writer's journal might contain a description of the dental hygienist, the dentist, or the dental office; a word picture of the writer in the dental chair, with an account of any discomfort experienced; or a description of the dentist's technique.

Should you be concerned if your child fictionalizes diary entries? Presuming she knows fantasy from reality, there's no harm in embroidering the truth or in making up entire scenes. In fact, these stories could well serve the purpose of freeing your child's creativity and allowing her to explore the delights of fiction writing in a completely safe context.

Here are some ideas to share with a child who's starting a writer's journal:

▶ Take a walk. When you get back, describe everything you heard.

▶ Describe the interior of the last restaurant at which you ate.

▶ Listen to a conversation between two people (students on the playground at recess?), then try to reconstruct it in your journal.

▶ To anchor your entries in historical time, include prices of movies and purchases.

▶ Choose a person you know well and describe him or her as completely as you can. Include both personality and physical traits. (What does the person look like? How does he or she act? Describe the person's laugh.)

▶ Make lists of all kinds: what you like best about yourself, your best friend, your school, your life; what you would like to do this year, next year, ten years from now.

▶ Imagine you're someone else, or an animal. Write an entry describing your feelings and actions as though you were that other being.

▶ Choose an event from your past. Begin by recalling and writing down every detail you can about the event, then go on to analyze how it has affected you in the present.

6. **The Family Journal.** All family members contribute to this chronicle of day-to-day activities and feelings. It's an open book for all to see, though at times the children's experiences may predominate. Anyone in the family feels free to inscribe details of what's going on in his or her life, or the life of the family as a group.

Examples: "Our family had an old-fashioned Thanksgiving get-together at the home of Aunt Em and Uncle Hubert, and Aunt Em showed everyone how to dance the polka...." "We picked out our own Christmas tree at a tree farm, and the tree almost feel off the car roof on the way home...." "We enjoyed a day in the snow, and baby Johnny tasted snow for the first time."

Most people write each entry from their own point of view, though I know one woman who delights in keeping individual diaries for her children, so that someday they'll have a record of their childhood activities without having gone to the trouble of writing it themselves.

Even things that seem dull and ordinary at the time will bring pleasure on re-reading years later. Everyday events take on a special quality when you reminisce about them together, when the children are growing or grown.

An alternative version of the family journal is a dialogue journal, in which two (or more) family members write inter-

actively, putting on paper what they might be reluctant to speak aloud. For some families, this is a good way to deal with problem situations.

● ● ● ● ●

Which kind of diary should your child try? One of them, all of them — it depends on your child. Different formats may be preferable at different stages of development.

At age eight, I recorded events in a homemade notebook. Between eleven and thirteen, I kept an almost-daily diary of events, with much mention of friends. At around fourteen, I began a diary in a steno notebook, in which I explored feelings in depth. (This is the diary I have kept up to the present day, although I use a computer now and I don't write as frequently.) At around the same time, I started keeping track of the many books I read by listing them in a notebook. When I was fifteen, I kept a "date diary" for rating boys. From age sixteen and into my twenties, I had a "moving diary," in which I recorded the major life changes that occurred each time I packed to move. At age seventeen, I kept a travel diary during a trip to Europe.

I introduced my son Simon to diary-keeping when he was four and a half, and the diary became a safe place for him to express his feelings. I would write whatever he dictated, whenever he wanted, then read it back to him exactly as he had spoken it. Soon he came to understand and trust that he had total freedom in his book, even to say silly things.

When I look back at my son's early entries, I realize that he was, in a way, writing to me rather than to himself. Sometimes what started as anger ended as mutual warm feelings. One entry began like this:

I am mad! Because I want Mommy to hug me and also because Mommy isn't nice to me and she won't help me. And because she's a grump!

A few lines — and a few minutes — later, he dictated this:

I want to say that everything is nice today and in fact that I love you and you are nice right now.

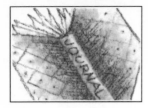

When I was ten and eleven, I downplayed the emotion in the events described below, possibly because my diary only had space for a few daily lines:

It is freezing today. Mom ran over my scooter while she was backing the car in the driveway.

The dentist was fun! It was a new one that we had not gone to before. I have only 3 or 4 cavities.

I am on the top line in the spelling chart. We had words from a sixth grade speller.

For the past few days I have been having strange emotional phases. I guess it's just signs of maturity. I was seemingly going mad over the fact I was alone. I was dying to be with boys.

Then, one week later:

I started menstruating today. One more sign that I'm becoming a young lady.

DIARY RULES

Actually, when it comes to your child's home diary, there are no rules. There are no teachers, no grades, no exams. It's absolutely okay to mix formats within a single book — for one day to be a "dream day," the next a "feelings day."

Complete sentences and perfect grammar are not essential. In fact, the effort required to achieve neatness and correctness can detract from depth, creativity, and completeness. Offer help with spelling and sentence structure only if your child asks for it. If your child seems to have the perfectionist (or revisionist?) urge to go back over entries and edit or rewrite them, discourage it. The diary is a process activity; the learning is in the freedom to be oneself. This aspect of diary keeping is especially valuable for those students who expect perfection of themselves in their schoolwork.

All topics are acceptable. For some people, writing about happiness is easier than writing about pain. Others only feel the urge to write when they are depressed or upset. To children who can't open up channels of communication or aren't ready to trust deep, personal questions to parents or anyone else, suggest using the diary as a "friend" who wants to be kept informed. Never imply any sort of obligation to write.

Reading the diaries of other people, especially of other children, may be the best inspiration for your child to begin her own journal journey. Find out what's available at your local library, including novels in diary format. Start by checking the resources below.

RESOURCES

The Creative Journal for Children: A Guide for Parents, Teachers, and Counselors by Lucia Capacchione (Shambhala Publications, 1989). Seventy-two writing and drawing exercises designed to foster your child's creativity, self-esteem, and learning skills. Children learn to observe themselves and exercise their imaginations, while forming the journal habit in a non-threatening way. Also recommended for parents is Capacchione's *The Creative Journal: The Art of Finding Yourself* (Ohio University Press, 1988).

The Days of My Life: A Journal for the Teen Years by Betsy Martin McMahon (New Chapter Press, 1987). For ages 11-18. Idea starters, imagination sparkers, and lined pages to help girls sort out their ideas, thoughts, and feelings in writing. Includes space for describing friends, teachers, guys, favorite music, dreams, regrets, plans, and much more.

The Diary of A Young Girl by Anne Frank (many editions). Gifted primary school-age children through adults can appreciate this classic. Pre-teens and young teens are especially able to relate to Anne's passionate emotions.

A Dog's Life: A Journal for You and Your Pet by Henry Horenstein (Macmillan, 1986) and *A Cat's Life* by Henry Horenstein (The Main Street Press, 1988). Books may be ordered from Pond Press. These are hardbound, 96-page pet journals, illustrated in color. A child could be creative and keep a diary as though written by the pet. Page headings include "The Early Years," "The Working Cat," and "The Happy Cat." Space for photos.

Families Writing by Peter R. Stillman (Writer's Digest Books, 1989). The family that writes together is a closer one, according to Stillman. He describes more than 60 imaginative, playful, and meaningful writing activities that can build links across generations, now and in the future. Included are ways to use words as gifts, how to record family

stories, fun with poetry, and how a computer might be right for your family. A pleasure to read.

Hannah Senesh: Her Life and Diary (Schocken Books, 1973). The Hungarian poet and freedom fighter began her diary when she was thirteen years old.

A Louisa May Alcott Diary, compiled and illustrated by Karen Milone (Little, Brown & Co., 1987). Calling itself a "scrap-bag" of things, this lockable book includes quotes from Alcott's books, stories, and journals; a calendar, crafts and activities; and topic and journal pages for inscribing thoughts and feelings. The topic pages open with a quotation followed by sentences to complete ("I made someone laugh when I…").

Mostly Michael by Robert Kimmel Smith (Delacorte, 1987). For ages 8–12. An eleven-year-old boy is given a diary and learns to enjoy writing about his growing pains. This warm-hearted story could motivate other boys to seek out the solace of their own private journals.

My Own Journal: An illustrated notebook (Running Press, 1989). Following an introduction which invites the child to feel free to write ideas, thoughts, feelings, and dreams, the pages are undated, lined on the left side of the page and blank (with only a small sketch at the top) on the right.

The New Diary by Tristine Rainer (Jeremy P. Tarcher, 1978). If you plan to inspire your child to begin journaling by starting a diary yourself, read this book for the complete how-to's. It includes helpful chapters on dream work, overcoming writing blocks, expanding your creativity, and transforming personal problems.

The Private and Personal Reading Journal of… (R.R. Bowker, 1989). This 16-page pamphlet, which includes quotes and amusing sketches, is for recording comments about books read. Space for 10 books.

Tell Me About Yourself: How to Interview Anyone from Your Friends to Famous People by D.L. Mabery (Lerner, 1985). For ages 10 and up. Information gained from conversations and interviews have a place in a writer's journal, and this volume teaches youngsters the basics of journalistic interviewing.

Then and Now: A Book of Days by Starr Ockenga and Eileen Doolittle (Houghton Mifflin, 1990). This unusual family keepsake contains a family tree to fill with photographs, and space for marking special events. Half of each monthly spread contains a photomontage guessing game with an array of characters.

Writing Down the Days: 365 Creative Journaling Ideas for Young People by Lorraine M. Dahlstrom (Free Spirit Publishing, 1990). For ages 12 and up. Creative suggestions for journal entries based on interesting things that happened in the past on that day, week, or month. Topics include celebrations, hobbies, historical events, science, sports, and games.

Writing for Kids by Carol Lea Benjamin (Harper & Row, 1985). For ages 8–12. Ideas to encourage youngsters to "put it in writing," including chapters on writers' notebooks and private journals.

CHAPTER 3

Don't Read This Chapter!

There must be some reason why the human brain contains at least ten billion neurons, each capable of transmitting nerve impulses via synapses to thousands of other nerve cells. Beyond the brain's workaday jobs of receiving sensory messages, controlling movement, and regulating body processes, this incredible organ lets us think and feel and imagine. It makes us human.

You can help build your children's mental powers by teaching them to think creatively and logically, and by discussing the differences between the two types of thinking. This chapter contains a variety of ways to exercise young brains and help children discover the delights of a rich imagination.

PARADOXES FOR KIDS

Don't read this sentence.

For you to have done as this sentence instructs, you must not have done as it instructs.

Paradoxes like this one are fun to share with young people. One definition of a paradox is "an argument that apparently derives self-contradictory conclusions by making valid deductions from acceptable premises." In other words, the information you're working with seems reasonable, and your logic is correct, but what you end up with just doesn't make sense.

Here are some more paradoxes to explore with your child:

▶ From the sixth century B.C.: Epimenides the Cretan said: "All Cretans are liars." Is he telling the truth? If so, he is lying...and so on.

Modern version: Say "I am lying." Are you? Then you aren't. Or are you?

▶ Say to a friend: "Answer yes or no: Will the next word you speak be no?"

▶ Am I asleep, or just dreaming I am?

▶ There are no errors on this page except this one.

▶ This sentence is false.

▶ Jason was disappointed that his Cub Scout meeting room had no suggestion box, because he wanted to put a suggestion in it about having one.

▶ Try this with a friend: Place a marble in one of two boxes, numbered #1 and #2, on a table. Say, "In one of these boxes, there is an unexpected marble. You may open them only in the order of their numbers. Which box contains the unexpected marble?"

If the friend opens Box #1 and the marble isn't in it, then it must be in Box #2, so it's not unexpected there. For the original statement to be true, it must be in Box #1, but then it's not unexpected there, either. So where is it? Perhaps in #1, perhaps in #2. Either way, it will be expected. Or will it? It's logically impossible to expect, at the same time, for the marble to be in both boxes.

▶ Can you imagine a map of the country drawn on a scale of 1 mile = 1 mile? Where would you spread it out to look at it?

▶ The only people I cannot tolerate are intolerant people.

▶ My son recently left the following outgoing message on a friend's answering machine, with her permission: "This is Kevin. I can't answer your call because I'm at home right now...."

▶ Print on one side of a card, "The statement on the other side of this card is true." Then print on the other side, "The statement on the other side of this card is false." The problem is, if you believe the first side to be true, then it must be false, yet if you assume it's false, it turns out to be true. This is called a self-reference paradox.

▶ Another kind of self-reference paradox is the endless sequence. This is what you get when you look into a mirror with another mirror.

Here's an endless sequence self-reference paradox that's popular with young children: "Pete and Repeat are on a boat. Pete falls off. Who's left?" At the obvious answer, "Repeat," the first part is repeated. (Caution: This can go on for quite a while.)

▶ Another self-reference paradox: "This sentence contains exactly threee errors." Is the sentence false, since it only contains two mistakes, or does that make the sentence itself an error, since it's false? If so, doesn't that actually make the sentence true? Is it false in order to prove it's true? Help!

▶ The concept of traveling through time offers a multitude of paradoxes, as anyone knows who has seen the movie, *Back to the Future*, and its sequels. For example: One reason you can't possibly travel back in time is that if you accidentally killed your own grandfather years before you were born, you never would be born (would have been born?).

Can your child imagine other complications of time travel?

▶ An oxymoron is a short paradox expressed in two words that seem to contradict each other. The word comes from the Greek oxy (sharp, pointed) and moron (foolish).

Examples: a soft rock, a loud whisper, a sad smile.

Can your child think of others?

▶ Come up with oxymorons that only make sense in your own family. For instance, I recently realized that to my book-collecting husband, the phrase "having too many books" is an oxymoron. In other words, he believes it's impossible to ha· too many books.

▶ Have you seen the bumper sticker that states, "Honk if you hate noise pollution"? Or heard the sentence, "I used to be indecisive, but now I'm not so sure"?

▶ *Omni* magazine once awarded a prize in their "new laws" competition to the originator of the so-called "Hofstadter's Law," which states, "It always takes longer than you expect, even when you take into account Hofstadter's Law."

▶ The drawings of Dutch artist M.C. Escher, including the famous one in which he shows hands drawing and being drawn by themselves, illustrate the notion of visual paradox. Many children enjoy Escher's drawings, most of which have been reproduced in books and magazines. Consider visiting your local library to explore some of these with your child.

■ ■

THE MÖBIUS STRIP: A VISUAL PARADOX IN 3-D

The möbius strip is an example of a "vicious circle" — a visual self-reference paradox. Your child can make a möbius strip by taking a strip of paper, giving it a half-twist, and taping or gluing the ends together.

When you follow its edge, the möbius strip seems to have only one edge and one side, even though that's impossible.

Draw a line down the middle of the outside of the möbius strip. What happens?

Now cut the möbius strip along the line. The result isn't two strips, but a single larger band.

■ ■

TOUGH QUESTIONS, ALIBIS, AND MORE MIND STRETCHERS

▶ *Parade Magazine* has a question-and-answer column called "Ask Marilyn." Readers direct questions to Marilyn vos Savant, who is listed in the *Guinness Book of World Records* under "Highest I.Q."

Here's a question that ran in the August 27, 1989 column: "If given an opportunity to choose, what is the most important choice that could be made in anyone's life? I think it would be to choose our parents, because they determine our environment." Marilyn's answer: It might be even better if we could choose our children.

Other questions from the column: "What do you think was the first word to be spoken?" (Marilyn believes it might have been "no.") "How come a psychic never wins a lottery?" (Marilyn's response: "Why don't psychics always win lotteries?")

Check out back issues of *Parade* and see how your child would answer some of these questions. Or work together to think of more to send in to vos Savant's column. Write: "Ask Marilyn," Parade, 750 Third Ave., New York, New York 10017. (Note that the column doesn't give personal replies.)

▶ Do the younger members of your family seem to use their most creative energies coming up with excuses for why they didn't do their homework or chores? Just for fun, suggest they devise a series of clever and far-fetched alibis. They can carry this further by making up excuses for historical figures or fictional characters.

Examples: "I didn't wash the dishes because there were sharks in the sink." "George Washington chopped down the cherry tree because he saw termites in it."

■ ■

YOUR FAMILY BOOK OF WORLD RECORDS

Immortalize each of your children's successes, however minute, subtle, or outrageous, by inscribing them in this unusual book. In a simple notebook, write the name of the child, the date, and his or her noteworthy feat.

Examples: Louis ate 19 lima beans, 9/3/90. Kelly did homework three days in a row without being reminded, 9/15/90. Samantha constructed a domino creation using 120 dominoes, 8/7/89. Bill thought up 52 uses for an old sponge, 8/23/90.

Virtually anything you or they can imagine qualifies for inclusion.

■ ■

▶ Compile one or more lists of things you would need to know about a person in order to really know him or her.

Examples: If you were planning to hire someone to work for you in your own business, you might want to ask about his work history, grades in school, hobbies, favorite activities, eventual career plans, and so on. But...

If you wanted to find out if someone would make good company on a long cruise, you might ask completely different questions — about her favorite book, movie, and TV show; neatness and sleep habits; how much quiet she likes; how many games she knows and enjoys; and so on.

Other questions you might include in this kind of inventory are: the person's age; favorite ice cream, color, song, toy, and snack; whether the person has brothers or sisters; pets; and so on.

▶ Imagine what kind of automobiles various historical figures would choose if they were alive today. (Accept all logic, even if far-fetched.)

Examples: My family thought of pairing Hitler with a Corrado (a Volkswagen), George Washington with a DeLorean, Abraham Lincoln with a Lincoln Continental, Howdy Doody with a wood-paneled station wagon,

Shakespeare's Richard the Third with a Porsche ("My kingdom for a Porsche!"), and Chief Cochise with a Cherokee (although Cochise was an Apache).

▶ Brainstorm a list of mistaken beliefs and carelessly held assumptions. Begin with the question "Do you have to… to…?"

Examples: Do you have to go to school to be smart? Do you have to be a girl to play with dolls? Do you have to be sad to cry? Do you have to work hard to be rich? Do you have to get caught to be a thief?

This exercise was suggested by The Stanley Foundation, which publishes teaching aids about global perspectives. For more information, write: The Stanley Foundation, 420 E. Third St., Muscatine, Iowa 52761. Or call (319) 264-1500.

▶ Educator and author Herb Kohl has found that asking students to list "Ten Ways Not to…" frees their creativity and helps them learn how to do a particular thing.

Example: Your son wants to learn to bake cookies. You teach him the basics, then ask him to come up with "Ten Ways Not to Bake Cookies." These might include: Be sure the oven is cold. Wrap yourself in foil. Stir dough with a banana. Eat half of the dough before pouring onto the baking sheet…

▶ Divide the world into "Two Kinds of People." There are many ways to approach this.

Examples: There are two kinds of people: those who spit out their gum, and those who swallow it…those who fold their toilet tissue into neat squares before using it, and those who crumble it first…those who put their toys away every day, and those who only straighten their rooms when they can't find something…those who measure how much salad dressing they pour on their salad, and those who don't…those who divide the world up into two kinds of people, and those who don't.

▶ Give a party in which guests are asked to come as oxymorons, contradictions, anachronisms, or something equally unexpected.

Examples: Dress as a fat flamingo...a New Year's baby with a cane...a very short basketball player...a baby with a mustache...a cowboy with a portable computer.

▶ Help your child to compile a travel guide to her own city, listing and annotating favorite attractions. Or she can design a walking-tour map of her own neighborhood.

She might begin by imagining that she's seeing the neighborhood through the eyes of a tourist. What would be worth visiting? Is there any local lore attached to certain spots?

Using a large piece of paper or poster board (available at any art supply store), draw the area with which your child is familiar. Sketch in the roadways and high points in pencil before drawing the final copy. Include personal notes: "This is where Mr. Jones, the crossing guard, is on duty every school day from 8 a.m. to 4 p.m." "This shop has a sale on gifts every Christmas." "This library offers story hours on Saturday mornings."

■ ■

AN EXERCISE IN BAD TASTE

Work with your child to create a "Book of Kitsch" filled with examples of bad or questionable taste. These can be cut from magazines or catalogs, or gathered from any other source.

Examples: A plastic purse in the shape of a banana...coasters with famous paintings on them...a Nativity Scene made of chocolate.

Of course, not everyone will agree on what is and isn't "kitschy." (One person's kitsch is another person's treasure.) For a variety of objects that most people would probably put in this category, request a copy of the Archie McPhee mail-order catalog, which features Fred Flintstone popsicle molds, fake rotten teeth, rubber chickens, big plastic feet, and much more. Write: Archie McPhee, Box 30852, Seattle, Washington 98103. Or call (206) 547-2467.

■ ■

▶ You've probably seen TV shows in which guests perform incredible or silly stunts. Brainstorm some stunts you'd like to see, even ones which are impossible to do.

Examples: Fold a pretzel, then carry it to Guam. Do a backwards double flip. Toss a car across a creek.

▶ Draw a "What's Wrong with this Picture?" picture. Choose a scene — your bedroom, the living room, your classroom, the grocery store — and imagine everything that could be wrong.

Examples: a cat in the fish tank, a TV remote control device in the baby's crib, books with their titles spelled wrong or with the wrong authors' names, a computer with the keys in an odd order, a pig opening the refrigerator.

▶ The ordinary balloon can lead to a number of creative insights in the hands of an imaginative child (past the age where choking on a broken piece of balloon is a possibility).

My son Kevin once pushed a penny into a balloon before blowing it up. It was interesting to see how it moved erratically around inside the balloon as he tossed it. Another time, he placed one balloon inside another. He blew the inside balloon up first and tied it, then the outside balloon.

More ideas: Draw a design on a deflated balloon with a marker and see if you can predict what it will look like when the balloon is inflated. Find out which of two balloons, one larger and one smaller, will make a louder noise when popped. (You might be surprised.)

▶ Buy a huge bag of jelly beans, chocolate chips, or popcorn, and fill a large glass jar. Get everyone in the family to guess how many jelly beans (or whatever) are in the jar. Then count them. Work on learning to estimate accurately.

CHANGE IT, FINISH IT, MAKE IT UP

▶ Remember the old "Believe It or Not!" columns, books, and TV shows? A number of years ago, a magazine called *New West* ran a humorous take-off on that idea called "McColly's

Take It or Leave It!" These consisted of "Amazing Frauds" (like a clown who disguised himself as a regular human being) and "Astonishing Feats" (like a kid who could go 53 miles per hour on a playground slide). Create your own versions of Amazing Frauds and Astonishing Feats.

▶ *New York* magazine once ran a weekly competition challenging readers to fill in the blanks in the sentence, "It was so _____ that _____." Here are two of the responses: "That Christmas tie was so loud that when I put it on the neighbors banged on the pipes," and "That building is so tall, they show movies in the elevator."

See if your child can think of more examples.

▶ Assemble a collection of cartoons (those from *The New Yorker* are especially good for this) and cut off or fold under the captions. Then devise your own amusing captions. Gagline is a commercial version of this game; see Resources, page 47.

▶ Devise new endings for familiar proverbs. First graders came up with these: Don't bite the hand that…is dirty. Eat, drink and…go to the bathroom. If at first you don't succeed…go play.

Examples: Don't count your chickens…Don't put all your eggs…People who live in glass houses…All work and no play…Children should be seen and not…You can lead a horse to water but…

▶ Rewrite the endings to common fairy tales.

Examples: Pinocchio might decide to keep telling lies and growing his nose long, then cut off parts of it to sell for firewood to support his family. Or the wolf in "The Three Little Pigs" might realize that brick houses are a terrific buy, stop bothering the pigs, and purchase several brick houses for investment purposes.

▶ Design your own holidays. Start by visiting your library to look through various "books of days," such as *A Dictionary of Days* by Leslie Dunkling (Facts on File, 1988), which describes over 850 named days.

"Daft Days" is a Scottish term for the days of merry-making at the New Year. "Maybe Tuesday" was invented by Peter de Vries in his novel *The Tunnel of Love;* on this day, TV crews would enter homes and take away some article of furniture if the owner answered a quiz question incorrectly. "White Stone Day" was named for the ancient Romans' habit of using a piece of white stone or chalk to mark particularly happy or fortunate days on the calendar.

Anyone in the family could come up with an apt name for a day of celebration or gloom, along with a particular way to commemorate it.

Examples: "Shuffle Shoes Day," when family members trade shoes…"Dead Caterpillar Day," when everyone gives each other "warm fuzzies" (says nurturing things to each other) and crawls around on the floor…"The Day After Birthday"…and so on.

▶ Invent a silly game. There are no rules, and no equipment is needed.

Examples: From *Graeme Garden's Compendium of Very Silly Games* (Methuen, 1987):

In "Quiche, Ratatouille, Avocado, Muesli," two players rotate a skipping rope over the playing area, and the skippers jump while chanting "olive oil, garlic, aubergine, langoustine." The first player to accidentally say "quiche, ratatouille, avocado, muesli" is eliminated.

In "Thrips," a game for three to seventeen players, each is required to impersonate a thrip (Graeme Garden facetiously recommends that you "consult any reliable book on the cultivation of roses, with particular reference to the section on insect pests"). The winner is whoever can maintain the impersonation for the longest time without falling over.

In "Hide and Squeak," guests at a party hide in the corners, and the host releases rats.

▶ Invent a new machine that does a better job of handling some everyday problem. Draw a diagram of the invention. Name it and write an advertisement describing it.

BOOK-INSPIRED BRAIN-BENDERS

▶ In Edward De Bono's *Children Solve Problems* (Penguin Books, 1972), children ages three to fourteen were asked to draw solutions to nine separate tasks.

Ask your child to solve these problems by drawing. Encourage the inclusion of detail.

1. Invent your own fun machine.

2. How would you go about weighing an elephant?

3. Design a bed that helps people get to sleep more easily.

4. How would you improve the human body?

5. Design a bicycle for mail carriers.

▶ Robert Fulghum, author of the bestselling books, *All I Really Need to Know I Learned in Kindergarten* and *It Was On Fire When I Lay Down On It* (Villard Books, 1988 and 1989, respectively), has developed what he calls "Fulghum's Recommendations." He describes them as being "less ironclad" than the Ten Commandments. They include such tongue-in-cheek suggestions as always to take the scenic route; to buy lemonade from any kid who is selling; and to be there when the circus comes to town.

Your child can make up his own "ten commandments," laws, recommendations, or rules for living.

Examples: "Never sit on a toilet without checking to see if the seat is down." "It's more fun to pay for fun before you have it than after." "If you put off writing a letter to a friend long enough, the other person will think it's their turn again."

▶ You may have seen books in the genre of *101 Uses for a....* Try brainstorming ideas for new books that contain 101 uses for...whatever.

Examples: 101 Uses for Used Coffee Cans, Toothpicks, Used Dental Floss, Broken Balloons, Dust, Broken Clocks, Brussels Sprouts...

If one or more of the titles is inspiring enough, your child may decide to write the book.

▶ Read and discuss E. A. Abbott's science-fiction classic, *Flatland* (Dover, 1952), which explores the life of a two-dimensional being in a 3-D world.

While the concepts are thoroughly entertaining, it's not a simple book, so if your child is young, you might read it yourself and explain it. You'll find it will open your youngster's mind to all sorts of questions about physics and relativity, even if she isn't scientifically inclined.

▶ Explain the concept of Utopia. Edward Bellamy's *Looking Backward* is a classic in the field, perhaps easier to follow than Thomas Moore's older version and others.

Talk about what the "perfect" society would entail, what your child would like it to contain, how the government would work, how such problems as poverty and illness would be handled, and whether any existing societies have come closer to this concept than our own. Discuss the drawbacks: What if people had different ideas of perfection? How would you handle dissenters?

What I remember, from reading this book in the seventh or eighth grade, is the question of whether it would be better for the government to put up one large continuous awning to act as a communal umbrella, or for people to carry individual umbrellas.

▶ Depending on your personal religious beliefs, you may enjoy discussing your ideas of heaven or hell. Try conversation-starters like: "If I could plan heaven, this is what I would have there…." "If I imagined hell, this is what I would see…."

▶ Peruse together some Books of Lists, such as those written by David Wallechinsky and family, or Sandra Choron's *The Big Book of Kids' Lists* (see Resources, page 13). Then develop your own lists. Use questions like these as starting points:

1. What are your six favorite foods?

2. Name four words with an unpleasant sound.

3. What are the five most beautiful words in English?

4. Make a list of the most outrageously dressed rock stars.

5. Who are the three people you'd most like to have spend the weekend at your house?

6. Which three books would you take with you onto a desert island?

▶ In *A First Dictionary of Cultural Literacy: What Our Children Need to Know* (Houghton Mifflin, 1989), E.D. Hirsch, Jr. has gathered what he believes are the most important facts every six- to twelve-year-old should know. He covers proverbs, literature, mythology, history, geography, math, the arts, and the sciences.

Work with your child to compile a booklet of "necessary information" for her age group.

▶ Dennis Beattie is soliciting whoppers for a book he plans to publish, called *Liars' Book of World Records and Astonishing Feats*. Among the tall tales he's collected so far are the ones about the woman who ran her 1989 Honda over 641 beer bottles before getting a flat tire, the man who bowled a 600 game, and the man who claims to be the world's tallest midget at six feet four inches.

Have fun with your child inventing some more tall tales.

IMAGINATION TOWERS

Decorating and populating "Imagination Towers" will keep one
to several children creatively busy for an hour or longer. All
that's needed are a few feet of butcher paper (or several sheets of
paper taped together on the back) and some colorful marking
pens or crayons. More than one "building" can be under con-
struction simultaneously.

Place the unrolled length of paper on a table or the floor, or
attach it to a wall. Draw the building's outlines using a ruler.
Make it at least four feet long (or high), with plenty of large windows. Extra touches such as a door, front porch, or roof can be
added at the start, or left to the whim of individual designers.

Say, "Pretend you can get close to each of the windows, so
you can see into the entire room. Imagine what you might see
in each of these rooms and draw it."

I've used this idea with children from ages five to thirteen
(you can join them when there are leftover windows). Some
children draw someone asleep on a bed, perhaps adding an
alarm clock ringing. In the next room we might glimpse a parent preparing breakfast. One child drew a pot overflowing and
smoking on the stove. Some children delight in expanding the
picture, adding kites and message systems (perhaps using ropes
and pulleys) that connect two or more tenants.

It's fun to add word balloons, cartoon-style, to give voices to the characters. There might be an argument in progress in one window or a party in another, with each guest making some comment to a birthday child.

What if through one window we can see the results of a bathtub faucet left running too long, and a partly open door showing the surprised face of an occupant returning to face a goldfish swimming in his bubble-filled apartment?

It's also possible to choose a futuristic setting for "Imagination Towers," say the year 2010. Or combine this activity with a history lesson and choose a time from the past.

RESOURCES

Absolutely Mad Inventions by A. E. Brown and H. A. Jeffcott, Jr. (Dover, 1970). Dozens of actual patented inventions, including a hat-tipping device and an edible tie pin. Illustrated.

Art Synectics: Stimulating Creativity in Art by Nicholas Roukes (Davis Publications, 1982). This heavily illustrated "teachers' guide" offers many easy-to-duplicate-at-home creative art and mental activities. Examples: Use clay or pen and ink to depict birds on a coffee break, or corn vs. carrots playing baseball. Visualize a chair made of ping-pong balls or a table made of flowers. Make a surreal totem out of 20 clear plastic drinking glasses filled with various objects, such as photos and miniature toys. By the same author: *Design Synectics* (Davis, 1988). This book has a great chapter on the paradox of art. Both *Art* and *Design* are for ages 10 and up.

The Complete Time Traveler: A Tourist's Guide to the Fourth Dimension by Howard J. Blumenthal, Dorothy F. Curley, and Brad Williams (Ten Speed Press, 1988). A comprehensive, 212-page examination of time travel in all its paradoxical impossibility, written as though travel through time were an everyday reality. A "gimmick book" carried capably through to the far limits of the imagination, it ranges across topics including working with a time-travel agent, the importance of accessories during time travel, why you shouldn't take children back to 1212 to visit the Children's Crusade, and so on. Includes an excellent appendix on the literature of time travel.

Family Words: The Dictionary for People Who Don't Know a Frone from a Brinkle by Paul Dickson (Addison-Wesley, 1988). An amusing compilation of words and expressions families have coined. Some are now in

common usage. ("Brinkles" are the marks left on your face by sheets or the couch when you wake up from a nap.)

Fantasy and Surreal Postcards: 24 Ready-to-Mail Photo-Collages in Full Color by Michael Langenstein (Dover, 1986). An example of amusingly applied creativity.

Flat Stanley by Jeff Brown (Harper & Row, 1964). For ages 7–10. Reminiscent of Kafka, this classic tale is about a little boy who wakes up two-dimensional one morning. He gets around, however, and even manages to foil some art thieves with his ability to impersonate a painting.

Gagline: The Unique Cartoon Caption Game. Players vie to create the most absurd, witty, and clever captions for captionless cartoons. The game includes four booklets, each containing the same 126 cartoons to try. (The original captions are also included.) Players vote for their favorites, and chips are awarded. Cartoons can be used as story starters, too. Write: Invisions, Inc., 815 N. Bundy Dr., Los Angeles, California 90049.

Gee, Wiz! How to Mix Art and Science or the Art of Thinking Scientifically by Linda Allison and David Katz (Little, Brown & Co., 1983). For ages 8 and up. This book shows that science is an art and a way of thinking about the world. In the process of finding this out, readers explore such topics as color, vision, symmetry, and physics.

Great All-Time Excuse Book by Maureen Kushner and Sanford Hoffman (Sterling, 1990). Funny excuses for every situation a child might encounter.

Hobble-de-hoy! The Word Game for Geniuses compiled by Elizabeth Seymour. This word-game-in-a-book is a version of "Dictionary," the traditional game in which players invent definitions for obscure words. The 1001 odd words are in one half of the hardcover book, while the other half contains their definitions. Recommended for three or more players, but two could develop their own variations. Write: Lime Rock Press, Box 363, Salisbury, Connecticut 06068. Or call (203) 435-9458.

How to Make a Zero Backwards: An Activity Book for the Imagination by Richard Kehl (Scholastic, 1989). For ages 6 and up. Suggestions for 15 imaginative art-related projects in which you do ordinary things in new ways. Color illustrations.

Illusions edited by Edi Lanners (Holt, Rinehart and Winston, 1977). Illustrated throughout, this volume covers every kind of paradox and visual illusion.

101 Amusing Ways to Develop Your Child's Thinking Skills and Creativity by Sarina Simon (Lowell House, 1989). For preschool to grade 3. Easy-to-implement, clearly explained activities in the following categories: logic and classification, reading and language arts, math, science and social studies, motor development and self-awareness, and art and creativity.

Supposes by Dick Gackenbach (Harcourt Brace Jovanovich, 1989). For ages 3–5. This picture book imagines and boldly illustrates the impossible: Suppose a polar bear had money, or a cow jumped into your bed…

Unusual Airplanes by Don Berliner (Lerner, 1986). For ages 8 and up. This book details all kinds of unexpected modifications to aircraft. A child with an interest in this subject might be inspired to create and invent on his or her own. Includes sections on planes with unusual wings, tails, fuselages, and powerplants, as well as the largest and smallest planes, the most and least powerful, and the most beautiful and ugliest.

Vicious Circles and Infinity: An Anthology of Paradoxes by Patrick Hughes and George Brecht (Penguin Books, 1975). A collection of paradoxes, from the ancient to the modern, including a section of photographs.

CHAPTER 4

Find Adventure in Ordinary Places

N o doubt you've already beaten a path between your house and every nearby place parents traditionally visit with their children. What's next? Surprisingly, your alternatives are not necessarily limited to repeating experiences or traveling great distances. The best opportunities for piquing your child's curiosity may still await you close to home.

Most family "education" trips — whether abroad, or to the local museum — target the exotic, with the purpose of transforming the strange into the familiar. But a whole new world is open to those who are willing to look through the other end of the telescope and see the familiar in an unusual way. So the next time you're facing a school vacation, or just another weekend that you hope to fill with adventure, consider the benefits of going someplace ordinary.

On each expedition, let your child's curiosity shape the activity. As Joanne Cleaver notes in her book, *Doing Children's Museums: A Guide to 225 Hands-On Museums* (Williamson Publishing, 1988), don't forget that the act of choosing among various activities is important. Some children want to look over everything quickly, then zero in on something that has caught their interest. With a younger child, it's often best to limit yourselves to thoroughly exploring only a part of any attraction.

Don't be overly concerned about following up the trip with detailed discussion, or extending learning through asking a lot of questions. Your child will give you the opportunity to help him learn by asking you questions. He may even ask for a return visit. And although you might prefer going somewhere new each time, a child often gets a deeper understanding from noticing details that were overlooked the first (or second, or third) time around.

WHERE TO GO AND WHAT TO DO THERE

▶ Attend an auction. Check the phone book and the classified ads in your newspaper for times and locations. Arrive early so you and your child can rummage through the "treasures." Auctioneers really do talk fast, so prepare your child.

- Spend a day at estate sales or garage sales (called "tag sales" in some parts of the country). Often these provide interesting glimpses into people's lives and lifestyles.

- Visit an animal shelter or humane society. The employees and volunteers will likely be eager to explain their jobs and introduce the animals.

- Explore the periodicals room of a major library. There you can view microfilms of old newspapers and, for a small charge, photocopy pages to take home. Go prepared to look up specific items, such as the front page of *The New York Times* on your child's birthday or the day Lincoln was shot. This glimpse into history is bound to be more interesting than most textbook accounts.

- Visit an antique shop or show. Allow your child to look around at her own pace. (For this, as for every adventure with your child, be prepared to spend time differently than you would if you were on your own.)

- Go to an airport (sometimes smaller airports are more amenable to tours). Notice differences in the angle of take-off for various sizes and kinds of planes. Stop in a waiting room to people-watch. Bring along a camera for picture taking from the observation deck.

- Visit the docks or a pier. Take a boat ride, and notice how the color of the water changes as you leave shore.

- Stop by the city or county office where real estate records are kept. Look up the history of your house or apartment building.

- Visit a military base. Air Force bases, for example, have free air shows. Afterward, discuss your views about war, peace, conscription, and military expenditures.

- Attend a coin show or browse around a coin shop, where your child will see things like pounds of gold or 2,000-year-old coins. He might want to start checking your loose change for rarities.

▶ Consider doing routine things at unusual times, and give your child a fresh perspective on the everyday.

Examples: Visit the beach in the rain. Walk through your neighborhood early in the morning. Arrive very early at a supermarket, when the produce is being unloaded. Try serving a hearty breakfast menu for dinner.

▶ Attend a dog or cat show. Find out how the animals are judged.

▶ Call on a bee keeper, a lapidary, a jeweler, a glass blower, a potter, a taxidermist, or another artisan who works close by. Phone ahead and find out if the person can show you and your child around and demonstrate some of the things he or she does.

▶ Arrange to have a tour of a radio or TV studio. Before you go, have your child watch or listen to a program whose set or stars you might see.

▶ Watch a class performing judo, yoga, karate, jujitsu, or drama. Visit such classes even if your child doesn't plan to participate (she may change her mind).

▶ Tour a factory, automobile assembly plant, police department, fire department, newspaper, or courtroom in session. Call to make reservations and to find out if there are age limits. Nearby communities may offer what your own does not. (Whenever you go anywhere, ask if your child can go behind the scenes: to see an airplane cockpit, theater dressing rooms, a hospital operating room.)

▶ Walk around the oldest part of your town. See what you and your child can learn about the history of your town by noticing dates on sidewalks and buildings.

▶ Watch a big computer in action at a local college. Find out what projects the computer is used for.

▶ Investigate your area's special resources. If you live near a dam, for example, you might be able to take a tour on which you literally walk under tons of water. Other excursions might include tours of water filtration works, fish hatcheries, milk-bottling plants, bakeries, even a chocolate factory.

▶ Visit the more offbeat museums and exhibits in your area; don't limit yourself to the usual circuit of children's, science, natural history, and art museums. Check under "Museums" in your local *Yellow Pages* for ideas. Some newspapers' weekend sections and city magazines list a wide variety of museums. Page through *America On Display* by Joyce Jurnovoy and David Jenness; see Resources, page 54.

    Examples: You may find airplane, railroad, or streetcar museums; firefighters' memorial museums; historical societies; interpretive houses; ethnic museums and societies; childhood homes of famous people, and other historic sites; sports halls of fame; museums started by private collectors (dolls, model trains, baseball cards, old telephones, musical instruments); ongoing special-interest exhibits; and more.

    A glance through one city's directory turned up this strange possibility: the "Questionable Medical Devices Museum."

▶ Keep on the alert for opportunities to see and do things you ordinarily wouldn't. Take a close-up look at the searchlight in the parking lot of the new shopping center. Watch workers strike a neighborhood carnival. Stop to see a bridge being cleaned, or a billboard going up. Follow hot-air balloons as they float overhead. Moments like these can be a child's most memorable experiences.

TAKE IN THE TRASH

▶ Gather up your recyclables — glass, aluminum, and/or newspaper — and take them to a recycling center. A huge mass of garbage about to be recycled makes an awesome sight, and there is much to learn about the hows and whys of recycling.

▶ Go to the city dump (don't remove anything unless it's allowed; usually it isn't). Before or after the trip, discuss with your child what you know about the garbage crisis.

▶ Walk around a junk yard. Perhaps you can find something your youngster is interested in fixing up (or further dismantling) at home. Take advantage of the chance to talk with your child about wants, needs, and our "throwaway society."

▶ Visit the place where cars are scrunched into scrap metal (an especially interesting experience after a trip to an automobile assembly plant). Compare the time, technology, and finesse necessary for creation with the brute force of destruction. You might also point out that many of the vehicles being scrapped "died" in accidents, not from old age.

RESOURCES

America on Display: A Guide to Unusual Museums and Collections in the United States and Canada by Joyce Jurnovoy and David Jenness (Facts on File, 1988). Offbeat museums are listed by region.

50 Simple Things You Can Do to Save the Earth by The Earth Works Group (Earth Works Press, 1989). This brief book contains several interesting and motivating sections on the whys and wherefores of recycling.

School's Out — Now What? Creative Choices for Your Child by Joan M. Bergstrom, Ed.D. (Ten Speed Press, 1984). Suggestions on how to tune into your children's special interests, and ways to help fill their free time creatively.

CHAPTER 5

Learning Comes Alive at the Cemetery

An unusual way to bring history alive for your children is to take them on cemetery visits. If they can read and understand the writing on the tombstones, they're ready for a memorable learning experience as they "dig" for information, perceive connections, and discover human stories.

You probably won't be alone, since more and more families and students of all ages are making field trips to cemeteries, as people used to do in poet Emily Dickinson's day. Whether their aim is to gain a healthier appreciation of death or to mine the wealth of historical lore, folks are finding that cemeteries are not scary places but oases of tranquility. Memorial parks are also unusually sensitive records of the changes each generation undergoes in its value systems.

PREPARING FOR YOUR VISIT

To locate cemeteries in your area, first try your local *Yellow Pages* under the heading, "Cemeteries and Memorial Parks." Your

Visitors and Convention Bureau will have information about the facilities most frequented by tourists, while historical societies will know of others.

You may also notice graveyards as you drive around town. Many are located in older neighborhoods or on the outskirts of metropolitan areas. Some are in churchyards, or in parks and grounds surrounding city, county, and state buildings. When traveling to other cities or countries, don't miss the local cemeteries.

Before your first visit, discuss the "ground rules" with your children. Explain that since other visitors may be at the cemetery to pay their respects to deceased loved ones, it's imperative that individuals conduct themselves with dignity. As long as your children stay on the paths (walking, not running) and speak in normal tones, they won't offend anyone. They don't have to whisper, but the general somberness of the place will probably help to restrain them from inappropriate behavior.

Bring along a note pad and pencil in case your children want to record some of the oddities they discover, make lists of names, or figure ages from birth dates. A magnifying glass may be helpful, too. And bring supplies for collecting rubbings, if your children are interested; see page 62.

Remember that most American children have very little first-hand exposure to death and its rituals. Your children's first impression is likely to be one of awe: So many people have died! Row upon row of tombstones, as far as the eye can see in all directions — like endless stars on a clear night — test one's vision of oneself as the center of the universe.

WHAT TO LOOK FOR: NAMES AND DATES

After finding out who owns and maintains the cemetery you've chosen to visit, begin your tour of the individual tombstones and graves. Think of your explorations as an attempt to unscramble a number of puzzles. Be sure your child understands what the common abbreviations stand for, such as "b." for "born," "yrs." for "years," and "dau." for "daughter."

▶ Talk about how people's names evolved from occupations, places of origin, and their parents' names. (Remind your child of where his name came from.)

- Notice how your town has changed ethnically over the years by comparing the last names on the older stones with those on more recent graves. What sort of ethnic mix can be seen?

- Focus on first names. What used to be the most common ones for men? For women? Are those names still in use? Can your child find any particularly unusual names?

- Are there any famous people buried in this cemetery? The owners may or may not agree to point out famous graves, but you and your child may come upon some well-known names on your own. In some communities, such as Hollywood, California, maps are available that direct tourists to the resting places of celebrities.

- Try to locate the stones at the opposite ends of time: the one with the oldest dates, and the one with the most recent dates. Talk about some of the things that have happened in the intervening years, decades, or centuries.

- Notice what sorts of accidents and diseases caused death in the past (when these details were more commonly inscribed into headstones than they are today).

▶ Compare gravestones of males and females to determine who lived longest. Did husbands outlive wives, or vice versa? Has adult life expectancy increased?

▶ How many deaths can be associated with childbirth? And what about child mortality rates? Mental figuring will enable your child to determine whether people died younger in past generations. Take this opportunity to discuss medical advances and improved health and sanitation practices.

▶ Is there a preponderance of headstones from one particular year? Work with your child to figure out why that might have happened. Could there have been an epidemic? A war? A natural disaster?

▶ Is there anything remarkable about the number of deaths by season of the year?

WHAT TO LOOK FOR: RELATIONSHIPS

▶ Looking at the tombstones of previous generations, what seems to have been the average number of children in a typical family? Do tombstones tell you anything about whether this number has decreased?

▶ What can your child deduce about changing family relationships by observing the patterns of the graves? How large did extended families used to be? What about today? Is it easy to find grandparents, great-grandparents, and grandchildren buried near one another?

▶ While colonial or early American gravestones usually represent only a single individual, the gravestones in modern cemeteries most often name two or more people, nearly always husband and wife. See how true this is in the cemetery you are visiting. Notice stones already engraved with the names of still-living spouses.

▶ Though this can be a bit complicated, it's also possible to determine changes in the ages at which men and women have married from one historical period to another.

Begin by choosing a family plot. Since you can assume that in most cases people had children not long after marrying, help your child figure out how old a particular child (or adult child) was when his mother or father died.

Example: If the father was born in 1880 and died at 40 in 1920, and the daughter was born in 1910, she was 10 when her father died. Subtract that 10 from 1920, or add it to the birth date of the father, to come up with the approximate age the father was when he married — in this case, 30. Of course, you will have to do this computation for a large number of families in order to come up with any sort of accurate determination of a trend.

▶ Compare the graves and headstones of the wealthy and the poor. These may be located near one another, in separate sections of the same cemetery, or in different cemeteries altogether. Discuss how a tombstone or marker can reflect a person's social status.

WHAT TO LOOK FOR: BELIEFS

▶ What can you tell about people's beliefs and values by the inscriptions on the gravestones? Talk a bit about how different religions view the possibility of an afterlife.

▶ Describe funeral customs of various societies and cultures throughout history.

Examples: The Egyptians practiced mummification, Romans generally preferred entombment, and the Vikings launched their dead in blazing boats. Hindus burn cast-off bodies on kindling pyres, and Muslims bury their departed lying on their right sides, facing Mecca. Also, Muslims don't use coffins, since they believe the corpse should be allowed to return to the Earth. Solomon Islanders have laid their dead on coral reefs as food for sharks; other Melanesians have eaten their late relatives themselves. The Irish hold wakes, and the Koryak tribe of northern Siberia play cards on the corpse. It's a Chinese custom to burn paper money at the graveside to ensure a happy afterlife for the deceased. And so on.

▶ Bone up on reincarnation and discuss it with your child. One eight-year-old girl, the daughter of a psychiatrist I

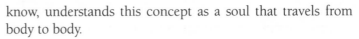

know, understands this concept as a soul that travels from body to body.

▶ If both of you feel comfortable doing this, brainstorm all the different ways people can die. Include a collection of far-fetched possibilities, such as death by tripping on a tombstone. Point out the next time your newspaper carries a notice of someone dying of a freak accident.

This activity doesn't have to be morbid. Use your best judgment of your own child's propensity to worry.

▶ Encourage your child to notice the variety of symbols engraved on the headstones. These may range from angels and lambs (especially on children's graves) to hearts, flowers, heraldic designs, and specifically religious symbols.

Discuss the meanings of these symbols. Common themes include the passing of time, the shortness of life, resurrection of the soul, and the occupation of the deceased.

Examples: Simply put, birds stand for the soul, trees for paradise or eternal life, angels for heaven, willow trees for mourning, trumpets for victory, anchors for hope, and snakes for rebirth. Crossbones show life's brevity. Also look for hourglasses (life passing), candles (life snuffed by death), crowns (glory and righteousness), bells (tolling for the dead), and fruits (fertility and abundance). On Jewish stones, hands open with touching thumbs signify that the deceased was a member of the priestly line. A compass with "V" symbolizes a member of the Society of Freemasons.

▶ If your visit coincides with a funeral, you may want to watch it arrive. Who arrives first? Notice the mourners' clothing, and determine what is considered proper behavior at such an event. What is the significance of the religious rites performed?

DIGGING DEEPER:
RELATED INVESTIGATIONS

▶ Budding geologists and casual rock hounds may enjoy finding the answer to questions like these: What kinds of rock are the markers made from, and why were these particular rocks chosen for this purpose? If the rocks aren't of local origin, where do they come from? Are different rock types used in different time periods? Do inscription styles vary by rock type?

Notice how many old gravestones tilt: Sections of soil settle at different rates. What effects have wind, rain (especially acid rain), and extreme temperatures had on the stones?

An interesting fact: Many nineteenth-century granite sculptors died from lung disease caused by exposure to granite dust.

▶ Like everything else, monument designs go in and out of fashion. You may find examples of the massive floral designs that were popular at the turn of the century, or Egyptian motifs that were in style in the 1920s. After the 1960s, a new freedom allowed quite a range of monument styles, while these days you're likely to discover very personal remembrances, from a surfboard to a color photo of the departed, encased in lucite and embedded in the granite. At some gravesites, you may even be greeted by the recorded voice of the deceased.

▶ Your child may enjoy collecting unusual epitaphs. Emily Dickinson called them "marble stories," and you'll find that these abbreviated biographies and autobiographies provide fascinating peeks into long-completed lives.

Perhaps your crew will come upon an inscription like the one on the gravestone of Mary Buell in Litchfield, Connecticut, which aptly illustrates how the Earth's population grows geometrically: "She died Nov 4th, 1768, at 90, Having had 13 Children, 101 Grandchildren, 274 Great G. Children, 22 Great G. G. Children, 410 Total, 336 survived her."

▶ An older child may enjoy making up her own "epitaph," perhaps including one or more versions of the inscription she imagines appearing on her own tombstone someday.

Distinguish between the extreme brevity necessary on a tombstone, and the leeway permitted in a newspaper obituary. Keep this discussion on the light side by injecting humor into it.

Examples: There was once a hypochondriac who had these words inscribed on his grave marker: "Now they'll

believe me!" The late comedienne Gilda Radner once wrote that when she died, she'd like to be buried with a working television. She wanted her tombstone to read: "Gilda Radner Program interrupted due to technical difficulties."

▶ Talk about which epitaphs were most likely chosen in advance by the deceased, and which were probably chosen by surviving friends or relatives.

▶ A cemetery is the perfect place to begin the habit of collecting rubbings. (Get permission from the proper authorities first.)

You'll need large, thin sheets of paper, masking tape, a fat wax crayon with the paper removed (or colored chalk), and a paint brush or whisk broom. (The broom is for cleaning off any dirt obstructing the words on the tombstone.)

To make a rubbing, tape the paper tightly over the chosen tombstone and rub the surface with the edge of the crayon until the stone's details show up sharp and clear. Be sure no tape is left behind when your child removes the paper. Have your child note the date and the name of the cemetery where the rubbing was taken.

▶ Many cemeteries have mausoleums, stone or marble buildings where the dead are stored above ground. Private family mausoleums are usually kept locked, but larger ones often are open to interested visitors.

▶ Some cemeteries contain buildings called columbariums, where the ashes of those who were cremated are kept. Explore these, too.

▶ Discuss all the people involved in the death of each person buried in the cemetery.

Examples: Did you mention the undertaker, member of the clergy, tombstone engraver, funeral director, embalmer, grave digger, cemetery maintenance crew, gardeners and security personnel, florist, caterer, casket maker, organist, coroner, cemetery architects and designers, doctor, newspaper writer, personnel in City Hall's Vital Statistics department, and sympathy card publishers?

▶ Talk about euphemisms that people in our society (especially cemetery and mortuary employees) use when speaking of the dead.

Examples: Cemeteries are "memorial parks," gravesites are called "interment spaces," dead people are "the deceased," people are "interred" instead of buried. Sales people who approach the public about buying cemetery plots work in the "before need" department.

▶ Notice the flowers. What kinds are found in cemeteries? Are there particular occasions or times of the year when flowers are left on many of the graves?

While you're at it, notice the "flowery" names for the avenues in some cemeteries: "Haven of Peace," "Slumberland," "Inspiration Slope."

RESOURCES

American Epitaphs, Grave and Humorous by Charles L. Wallis (Dover, 1974). Contains a collection of 750 authenticated epitaphs, many funny, some sad. Interesting historical sidelights and lessons are interspersed between the lines.

Best of Gravestone Humor by Louis S. Schafer (Sterling, 1990). A new collection of hundreds of amusing "last words."

Famous Last Words and Tombstone Humor by Gyles Brandreth (Sterling, 1989). Hundreds of examples of parting words and epitaphs.

Fred Hunter's Historical Funeral Museum, 6301 Taft St., Hollywood, Florida 33024. This unusual museum, which opened in 1987, shows how funeral customs have changed with our society. Exhibits dating back to the early nineteenth century include caskets, portable embalming boards, supplies from the days when embalming was performed at home before laying the body out in the parlor, memorial jewelry made from generations of dead family members' hair, and antique hearses. For more information, call (305) 925-8585.

Permanent Californians and *Permanent New Yorkers* by Judi Culbertson and Tom Randall (Chelsea Green Publishing, 1989 and 1987, respectively). Illustrated with maps and photographs of the gravesites, these

books provide guided tours of interesting cemeteries, featuring details about the lives and last resting places of hundreds of celebrities. Also in the series: *Permanent Parisians.*

Underfoot: An Everyday Guide to Exploring the American Past by David Weitzman (Charles Scribner's Sons, 1976). The chapter on "Resting Places" is quite detailed and includes a discussion of symbolism.

CHAPTER 6

Photography: More Than Meets the Eye

G ive your child a camera, and he or she will have the perfect tool for investigating the interesting, inspirational, and amusing scenes in your home and around the neighborhood. Taking pictures is an excellent way for young people to become actively involved in looking at and thinking about places, people, issues, and things. No longer a passive observer, but a participant in and recorder of the pageant, your child will gain much more than technical skill.

Self-esteem is enhanced when children operate a camera, since they are the decision-makers in charge of selecting the photo site, composing the shot, and posing the subject. Science enters

the picture, too, as children learn about lenses, apertures, and what film to use for what light.

Photography also offers a uniquely personal means of communication, which can be of special benefit to the less verbal young person. As some writers feel most free to express themselves while "hidden" behind their written words, photographers may open up most comfortably behind their cameras.

■ ■

PICTURES B.C. (BEFORE CAMERA)

A young child's first picture doesn't have to be made with a camera. You can work together to create sungrams, or shadow images. Sungrams are made by placing objects on photosensitive paper and exposing the paper to sunlight.

This technique introduces a child to the concept of negative images. It's a good first exercise in composition, because a child must create an original design for "photographic" reproduction. Sun-picture kits are available in craft stores for a few dollars.

■ ■

EQUIPPING THE YOUNG SHUTTERBUG

Even the youngest child will enjoy a "regular" camera. A toy camera can give satisfactory results, but since film and processing will be your most costly outlay over time, it makes sense to invest in a serious camera that produces consistently good photos. A first camera needn't be expensive or complex.

What about instant picture cameras, such as those made by Polaroid? While they enable a child to compare intentions with results immediately, less expensive pocket cameras will do more to develop a photographer's eye, and waiting a few days to have film developed shouldn't be a problem. Of course, you can occasionally go to the extra expense of having film processed at a one-day or one-hour processor.

If you own a 35mm camera, consider letting your child try it out. Usually, youngsters are either fascinated by the challenge and pursue it intrepidly, or they are intimidated by it and return happily to a simpler camera. For between $100 and $200, you can purchase for your youngster an auto-focus 35mm camera made by Minolta, Vivitar, Canon, Olympus, Nikon, or another well-known manufacturer. Some models now come equipped with such extras as zoom lenses. For most of these, the photo quality is surprisingly good, and mistakes are hard to make because exposure settings are fully automatic.

Auto-focus cameras are of great value for the young and perhaps impatient beginner, who can concentrate on the art of composing the shot, instead of on the technical side of figuring out lighting and distance. Still, if a child shows interest in moving beyond snapshot proficiency, she should have a camera with manual capability. If you can spend several hundred dollars, consider buying a single-lens reflex (SLR) camera, since these allow you to change lenses for greater flexibility.

Avoid flash bulbs and attachments; there's plenty to take pictures of in well-lighted places.

Which film is best for the new photographer, color or black-and-white? Each has its pros and cons. Black-and-white requires the photographer to think about fewer variables while shooting, though many professionals prefer it because of its artistic possibilities. It's cheaper to purchase than color film, but may end up being more expensive to have developed at the drugstore-type locations that send their film to huge laboratories, which do the bulk of their work with color. You'll often find discounts and coupon specials for color developing, but rarely for black-and-white.

Buy your film at discount stores and keep extra rolls in the refrigerator. Until your child's eye becomes more discriminating, have the film developed through your local drugstore or market. The quality will be adequate, and the cost will be much lower than at camera stores and photographic studios.

GETTING STARTED

When you introduce photography to children, don't try to turn them into instant experts, and be especially slow to criticize their results. The point, at least at the beginning, is to encourage visual literacy and to turn kids on to images. Your child's

vision will be different from yours. He may find something worthy in a weed patch, a pile of trash, an old car. Or you may find something aesthetic in these things, and he may not. Art is personal and unpredictable.

As I was looking through a collection of prize-winning photos from a variety of magazine contests, I came across the following photo subjects: someone behind a wet windshield, an old building, empty wet deck chairs, a sunset over a lifeguard shack, a child drawing with chalk in the street, rooftops, trees in autumn, an old barn, half a red car, an iron and ironing board, bicycle spokes, the sole of a shoe, a kitchen chair, eggs on three plates, brooms leaning on a wall, a fence, a cat, a man feeding pigeons, and the reflection of clouds in a puddle.

When you first hand your child a camera, and before you load film into it, have her open it and look through the back. Show how, when you manipulate the aperture ring in the front, she can see it open and close through the back of the camera. Do this before even mentioning shutter speed. Compare it to how we squint when we go out in the sun, and open our eyes wide in the dark. Let your child turn the aperture ring and look at the numbers.

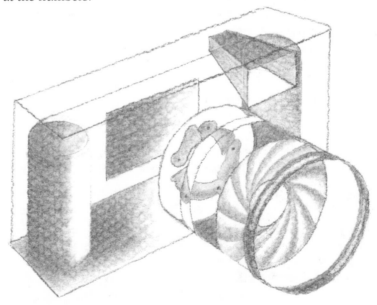

When discussing ISO (formerly ASA) numbers, keep the explanation simple. Use the analogy of a 100-watt bulb providing more light than a 50-watt bulb: The darker the room, the more watts you need. The higher the ISO, the more light the film attracts; that's why ISO 400 film is better for darker surroundings than ISO 200.

Allow lots of experimentation. It's not unusual for professionals to shoot one or more rolls of film to end up with one really satisfying photo. Help your child figure out where the less successful shots went wrong (if he's interested).

Most beginners simply "take" photos. They wait for the subject to present itself, and then they shoot a picture of it. Once that becomes less interesting, "creating" photos is next. This can mean staging a photo by telling the subject what to do, or it might mean using props.

Children often need assistance eliminating undesired elements from their photo compositions when they frame the shot through the viewfinder. Winifred Meiser, executive director of Through Children's Eyes, a Van Nuys, California-based nonprofit corporation that teaches photography to gifted and talented schoolchildren, explains her approach: "I have them take a picture — and then I put my finger over the tiny person in the photo, and I ask them what else is in their picture. I ask them what they were thinking about when they took the shot."

■ ■ ■ ■ ■ ■ ■ ■ ■ ■ ■ ■ ■ ■ ■ ■ ■ ■ ■ ■

THIRTEEN TIPS FOR YOUNG PHOTOGRAPHERS

1. Plan your photo before you press the shutter release. Keep it simple, with one center of interest (which doesn't always have to be in the center of the picture).

2. Look at what's in the background. Is it cluttered? Too busy? Is that what you really want to photograph? If not, move.

3. Hold the camera as steady as you can, especially when gently squeezing the shutter release.

4. Watch out for fingers and camera straps blocking the lens.

5. Subjects who look stiff and posed aren't as interesting as relaxed subjects and people in action.

6. Close-ups are often more interesting than distance shots.

7. Practice using the viewfinder so you don't cut people's heads off.

8. Try shooting the same picture from different angles and distances. See which turns out best.

9. Don't angle your shots too much. When you get them printed, it will look as if everything is sliding off the paper.

10. Don't let lamps, trees, and poles appear to grow out of people's heads. Shoot from a different position.

11. Beware of glare from mirrors, windows, and picture frames. Move to the side and shoot your subject at an angle.

12. Take a tip from many professional photographers: Keep a simple log as you shoot rolls of film. For each picture, make a note of the date, the subject, and anything else you might want to remember later. Or wait until your pictures are developed, then write the month and year on the back of each print.

13. Store your photos carefully. The easiest way is in three-ring albums with "magnetic" sheets — the sticky ones covered in clear acetate. These accept prints of all different sizes and allow for frequent rearranging.

Photos can also be stored in various kinds of boxes, including small plastic or metal file boxes.

■ ■

MASTERING THE MEDIUM

▶ Urge your child to use the camera to view things from unusual angles — close up, from above, through trees. Start in and around your own home. Look for textures and patterns in the walls of your house, in fences, in pavement.

Examples: "If I lay on my belly in the grass, I see a forest through the lens." "Your shoes would make a great picture. Pretend you're about to squish me — I'm a bug with a camera!"

▶ Encourage your child to view the same potential subject from a distance (long shots), from close up, and from a medium distance. The resulting photos will each emphasize a different aspect of the "story."

   Example: Try a long shot of baby brother playing in his room, a photo of the baby which contains only his face and body, and a close-up of his hands on a toy.

▶ Experiment with light. Direct midday sunlight has a bright, harsh quality, often forcing your subjects to squint. Sometimes results are more pleasing on overcast days, late in the afternoon, or early in the morning. The angle of the light affects the photo's depth and definition.

▶ If your child knows how to set an f-stop and shutter speed, have him take several versions of the same photo, keeping a record of which settings he used. Later, analyze the results with him. Find out what he does and doesn't like about each of his photographs.

▶ Open your child's mind to the possibilities of personalized picture taking.

   Example: Suggest that she limit herself for a week or a month to taking photos of the outside of your home in all kinds of lighting and weather conditions. She doesn't have to shoot the whole house, but maybe one brick, a section of siding, a step, part of the garden, or a window.

▶ Have your child and a friend of the same ability level each take a roll of photos of the same scenery. Compare the results. This is a good way to help your child grasp how individual the photographic eye is.

PICTURE THIS: PROJECTS TO TRY

▶ Write a story or a nonfiction article and take photos to illustrate it. Or take the pictures first, then write about them.

▶ Create a photo essay. Tell a story or illustrate a process using only pictures.

   Examples: Decorating a Christmas tree, baking a cake, refinishing a cabinet, cleaning out a garage.

▶ Create a photo diary. Carry a camera around for a day or for several days, snapping pictures of family members. Try to catch everyone doing something characteristic, and something out-of-the-ordinary.

Examples: The family eating a meal, little brother bathing, Daddy brushing his teeth, Mommy paying bills, the family pet frolicking, the child's own bedroom in its normal disarray.

The diary might also include snapshots of the mail carrier, the gas station attendant, and others who are a part of a day's events. Don't forget to take a photo of your young picture-taker to round out the diary.

▶ Suggest to your child that she try out unusual backdrops for her photos.

Example: Create an interesting effect by placing an object on the surface of a large mirror on the floor. Include both the object and its reflection in the shot.

▶ Draw a large picture using sharp, contrasting colors, then snap a photo of the artwork.

▶ Make photo books with a theme. These can be as simple or as complex as your child chooses.

  Examples: One book could include only pictures of items beginning with the letter B: book, baby, bottle, bird, bread. Another could be filled with examples of nature to be found in the city.

▶ Brainstorm together for creative book ideas.

▶ Go to the zoo, camera in hand. A purposeful approach to looking at the animals may kindle new interest in an activity that has become mundane.

  In fact, take a camera along on trips of all kinds. What used to be routine may become new — "Was that there last time? I never noticed it before."

  It may seem pointless to take photos of scenes already available on postcards, but kids like to do it. So buy the postcards, too, and make comparisons. Where did the photographer stand to get that shot? What time of day was it, and what season? What makes the postcard picture different from the photo?

▶ Visit the older neighborhoods in your town to photograph interesting architectural features such as roofs, windows, porches, and cornices.

▶ Compile a large community "map" composed of photos of favorite stores and other neighborhood haunts.

Ralphe

▶ Put together a "career album" of photos of people in your community doing their jobs. Include teachers, mail carriers, shopkeepers, police officers, fire fighters.

▶ Combine cooking and photography by taking photos of completed culinary successes, then filing them with the recipes.

▶ When photographing the family pet, get down to its eye level. Attract the pet's attention and get it to look alert by crinkling paper or showing one of its favorite toys. (This is also a great way to photograph a very young baby brother or sister.)

▶ Your child may enjoy the double pleasure of combining gardening and photography. Suggest that he crouch down so his subjects (flowers, for example) are at eye level. Either fill the viewfinder with lots of flowers or zero in on a single stem or blossom.

When the sun is low in the sky, sunlight from behind or to the side of a flower will emphasize its translucence. For a dewy, early-morning look any time of day, spray the flower with an atomizer before shooting it.

▶ Is your child a collector? Suggest that she start a photographic collection focusing on one particular thing.

Examples: Sunsets, clowns, architectural oddities, dogs, fountains, fire hydrants, donut shops, door knobs, playground structures. With a photographic collection, the only constraints are the limits of one's imagination.

▶ Draw or otherwise create backgrounds for stuffed animals or other toys, then photograph the scenes.

▶ Teach your child the meaning of the words "symmetry" (similarity of form on either side of a dividing line, harmony, balance) and "symmetrical" (balanced or similar on both sides, well-proportioned, well-arranged). Have her search out and photograph symmetrical images: a butterfly, two chairs facing a table, windows on either side of a door.

▶ Compile an "emotions album." Two or more children working together can pose to illustrate every emotion they can imagine — anger, joy, sorrow, puzzlement, and so on.

▶ "Mystery photos" are fun to take and share. The photographer chooses something familiar to photograph but tries to find a way to show only part of it, or shoots it from an angle that makes it look mysterious.

Try this with a common household object, an item of clothing, or something stored in the garage. See if family and friends can guess what it is.

TAKE A SCIENCE SAFARI

Bring along a camera on a scientific expedition outdoors. Here are some ideas to try:

▶ Take photos that show gravity at work.

▶ Find and photograph animal homes — burrows, hives, nests, even dog houses.

▶ Document the impact of people on the natural scene. How about a collection of "trash" photos?

▶ Catch evidence of animal life — feathers, tracks, droppings.

▶ Pretend you're a toad, a worm, or a bird, then take some photos that show how you see the world.

▶ Create "photo comics." First, think of a story (it needn't be funny) and write a script. Then combine the script with a plan of exactly what pictures you'll take. Get some friends or family members to act out your story while you take the photos. Vary your angles and distances.

After the photos are developed, arrange them and glue them onto heavy paper or cardboard. (You can also trim them any way you want. Many photos can be improved by cropping, or using scissors to cut away a boring or distracting background.)

Finally, write your dialogue on little "bubbles" of paper (or self-stick labels) and attach those to the photos.

▶ Your child can choose a poem he likes, then find a subject or scene to photograph which shows the mood of the poem.

■ ■ ■ ■ ■ ■ ■ ■ ■ ■ ■ ■ ■ ■ ■ ■ ■ ■ ■ ■

MAKE A BOOK OF CHANGES

Parents and children can work together to chronicle things that change over a period of time. Long after you think you're done with this, your child's sharpened awareness of her surroundings will keep resurfacing. Possible subjects for "before-and-after" photos include:

▶ empty lots with "_____ TO BE BUILT HERE" signs, followed by whatever is finally built

▶ old-building-to-new-building developments, including under-construction shots

▶ rivers at high water and low water

▶ oceans at high tide and low tide

▶ the same tree during the different seasons

▶ a carrot top, sunflower or other seed before planting, during growth, in full bloom, and wilted

▶ babies or toddlers at monthly or yearly intervals

▶ shopping areas or schools when they are crowded and when they are empty

▶ the price sign at a local gas station every few weeks

▶ an arrangement of favorite personal items chosen and periodically revised

■ ■ ■ ■ ■ ■ ■ ■ ■ ■ ■ ■ ■ ■ ■ ■ ■ ■ ■ ■

▶ For a more advanced project, try composing "trick" shots.

   Examples: Focus on a shoe poised menacingly above, or a toy car made to seem full-scale by its setting, or a toy animal posed with a mirror set up vertically between it and the camera to create a "two-headed" look.

   Even if the results are disappointing, they are still instructive, giving your youngster the stimulus for choosing, planning, analyzing results, and comparing intentions with outcomes.

▶ Try some "photo-fakery." A few years ago, a *Science Digest* contest challenged readers to create photos in two categories: UFOs and weird beasts. For UFOs, it was suggested that you throw a pie plate or a hubcap in the air. For weird beasts, possibilities include creatively decorated clay figures, double exposures of animals and people, and unusual shadows.

WHAT TO DO WITH ALL THOSE PHOTOS: CREATIVE POSSIBILITIES

▶ If your child has photographed simple objects — balls, apples, cups, boxes, flowers — suggest that he try drawing a picture using a photograph as a model.

▶ Choose a special photo to have enlarged to 8" x 10". Paste it on a piece of cardboard and cut it up into puzzle pieces.

▶ Create a bookmark using a photo, perhaps adding a written message. Have it laminated.

▶ Use a nature photo to decorate a wooden box, then coat with clear spray.

▶ Make a collage using pieces of photographs and bits of magazine illustrations, with or without words cut from advertisements.

▶ Assemble a family "photo tree" from pictures taken at family get-togethers. This might be part of a family history book including transcribed interviews with various family members.

▶ Make frames out of poster board, box lids, twigs, fabric over cardboard, and anything else you can think of.

▶ Make "photo puzzles" out of wooden children's blocks and glue. Crop six photographs into 5" squares. Cut each photo into four 1 1/4" squares. Glue each square onto a different block. Turn each block to the next surface and do the same thing with the rest of the photographs. When you're through, you'll be able to manipulate the blocks to show off your original six photographs.

PHOTOGRAPHIC SIDE-TRIPS

▶ Become a collector of props — items you can use to enhance photographs.

Examples: Costume jewelry, clothing, masks, stuffed animals, hats, eyeglasses, toy cars.

Once you're in the habit of seeking out such materials at garage sales and elsewhere, you may get a great picture idea just by spotting some unusual prop.

▶ Photography has been around for 150 years, and older children may find its history fascinating. Some of the art's most famous twentieth-century practitioners include Alfred Stieglitz, Edward Steichen, Edward Weston, Walker Evans, W. Eugene Smith, Henri Cartier-Bresson, Diane Arbus, and Imogen Cunningham. Check your local library for books highlighting their imaginative works.

▶ Read community calendar listings for photographic events and take your child to exhibits, museums, and photography centers. Outings like these motivate a youngster to experiment.

▶ Visit a photographer's studio or a friend's home darkroom. Ask questions: How is retouching done? What special techniques are used to produce unusual photographs?

If possible, visit a photographic laboratory where photos are developed and printed. Ask: How are slides developed? How are photos enlarged? What chemicals are used and where do they come from?

▶ Study the editorial and advertising photographs used in various publications. Determine what idea or message the photographer was trying to get across.

NEW USES FOR OLD PHOTOS

▶ Pull out old family albums and study the photographs with your child. You can learn a lot about a person or an era from the things people chose to be photographed with and the ways they posed.

Are the people dressed up or casual? Are they involved in work or leisure pursuits? Are they smiling? Are pets included? Are cars or perhaps horses given a front-and-center position? Are small children held on parents' laps or shown in natural poses? Notice the houses in the background. Or, if the photos were taken indoors, what rooms can you see?

I once purchased a whole box of old photographs inexpensively at an antique shop. Though we didn't know the people involved, it was still fascinating to look for clues to their personalities in the unlabeled photos.

▶ As you examine old photographs, remember that a single photograph can raise many questions. Some can be answered by the photo itself, but others require additional research. Be wary of jumping to conclusions from insufficient information.

Examples: A portrait of a man shows him holding a book. Does this mean he was an avid reader? Maybe and maybe not; perhaps the photographer posed him that way. Or: A portrait of a woman seems stiff and expressionless. Does this mean that she had a rigid personality or never showed emotion? Not necessarily. In the past, before fast-action cameras and film, taking a photograph took a long time. People had to sit absolutely still, often in uncomfortable positions. Because photographs were expensive, being photographed was a special event, and people thought they should look serious and formal.

▶ Use a magnifying glass to study old photos closely, item by item. Pay attention to details like clothing decoration, facial expressions, foliage, the lettering on signs and posters, the newness of a steam locomotive or automobile.

The interested child will likely ask questions about what she sees. Try to have resources on hand, like old mail-order

catalogs (for dating the style of dress) and an atlas or travel guide (for learning more about where the photo was taken).

PHOTOS THAT MOVE: VIDEO CAMERA FUN

If you own a video camera, your children have access to an art form that provides instant gratification as well as numerous learning opportunities. Because feedback is fast and easy — just pop the cassette into the VCR — technical skills can improve quickly.

Many of the activities suggested in this chapter for use with a still camera work just as well with video. Here are more ideas to share with your budding cinematographer:

▶ Start simply. The best way to learn the basics of what your family's video camera can do is by taping a casual event — a backyard picnic, a basketball game.

Show your child how to operate all the controls and let him try everything. Encourage him to experiment with fade-outs. Remind him to move slowly and not to zoom and pan too much.

Teach your child to limit individual scenes to fifteen seconds or so, instead of pointing the camera endlessly toward the same group of people doing the same thing.

Remember, his questions and your instructions will both be recorded on the sound track.

▶ If you've ever thought of making a video inventory of your family's household belongings (very useful for insurance purposes), consider letting your youngster do the job.

▶ Do you have favorite relatives who live far away? Perhaps your child can tape an extended message for them. This might include scenes of everyone in the family doing something characteristic, and family members speaking directly to the distant relative.

▶ Have your child tape "stories" instead of just pointing and shooting. This creates an awareness of plot, continuity, pacing, and the relative importance of events, all of which makes for more interesting videos.

Examples: The story of "how we all got ready for Jamie's surprise party," or "the day of the big soccer game," or "Thanksgiving at Aunt Sally's house."

▶ Carry this idea further: Invite your child to create a story. He can get together with friends, write a simple script, gather props, design titles, dress up, and act, then invite family members to the premiere.

▶ If your video camera doesn't have a character generator, your child can write her own titles with a wide felt-tip pen on cardboard. Film these at the start and at various points during the taping for a more polished look.

▶ Work together to make a documentary about baking cookies, planting a garden, or even something as mundane as cleaning the house.

▶ Choose a family member as subject and tape his or her typical day. Include footage of teeth brushing, aerobics, bed making, eating, and so on, and consider staging some special events (subject receiving something exciting in the mail? an animated telephone conversation?).

A pet can also be the subject of a day-in-the-life documentary.

RESOURCES

Developing the Creative Edge in Photography by Bert Eifer (Writer's Digest Books, 1984). Clearly written, enthusiastically described tips to motivate the photographer who is ready to move beyond the basics and become really good. Readers are told how to think creatively, how to capture mood and emotion, how to use the camera's controls effectively. Sharp 10-year-olds should be able to benefit.

The First Photography Book by Peter Smith (Sterling, 1987). A fully illustrated book of basics for beginners, including how to photograph stars, fireworks, and pets, plus how to reproduce photos on T-shirts.

For Your Own Protection: Stories Science Photos Tell (Lothrop, Lee & Shepard, 1989). For ages 8–12. An unusual angle on photography: By using scanning electron micrographs, thermograms, and high-speed strobe photos, the author shows how the human body is protected from environmental threats.

Four free or inexpensive booklets from Kodak:

▶ "Kodak Self-Teaching Guide,"

▶ "Self-Teaching Guide to Using a 35mm Camera,"

▶ "Teaching Tips from Teachers," and

▶ "How to Decorate with Photographs."

The first two booklets provide space for the photographer's own photos. Write: Eastman Kodak Co., Department 841, 343 State St., Rochester, New York 14650-0608.

My First Camera Book by Anne Costick (Workman, 1989). For ages 4–7. A teddy bear explains photo basics, and a 12-page first photo album is included in the book. A tiny reusable camera (which uses 110 cartridge film) is part of the package.

Trick Photography: Crazy Things You Can Do With Cameras by Robert Fischer (Evans, 1980). Eighty photographs and diagrams show and tell how to perform more than 60 trick shots.

CHAPTER 7

Use Your Head: Physical Activities that Exercise the Mind

Most children enjoy playing sports and games, and the benefits aren't only physical. Studies have shown that participation may enhance their overall intellectual development as well. Yet for some bright youngsters, the thrill of traditional physical activities can pall quickly. To keep your children from becoming sedentary specimens, it's smart to combine physical exertion with a healthy dose of mental stimulation.

This chapter has dozens of ideas for your whole family to try.

NEW GAMES

One way to put the fun back into competitive sports and games is by changing them into cooperative endeavors. Though the "new games" movement has been around for several years, most schools still teach physical education as though winning were all that mattered. As you and your child will discover, game-changing can be a liberating experience.

In *The Well-Played Game* (Doubleday, 1978), Bernard De Koven suggests that a good game is one in which all players are fully engaged by the playing, not by the need to win. A good cooperative game also includes these five elements:

1. A sense of humor (players laughing with each other)

2. Fun in the playing (not in keeping score)

3. Players feeling better about themselves during and after the game (no put-downs, no evaluations in front of the group)

4. Opportunities to be spontaneous and imaginative (players have a chance to change the rules)

5. Challenge and a sense of adventure.

Some children initially resist the switch-over from competitive to cooperative sports, thinking that play is pointless without a clear winner. If this happens with your child, talk about it. You might mention that competitive sports still have a place, but that designing and playing "the other kind" can be mind-expanding and helps to prepare one for a world that often rewards flexible thinking. On a practical level, try these tips: Play *with* them to show how it's done and how much fun it can be. Choose challenging games for older children used to competition. Suggest they simply try it to see if they like it, and don't push.

Here's a sampling of games for you to try, suitable for a variety of ages.

▶ "Brussels Sprouts" is a tag game invented by Pamela Kekich and described in *Playfair* (see Resources, page 99). "It" chases someone in slow motion, catches the other child, links arms with him or her, and they become "it" together. The next person captured also links arms. "It" becomes larger and larger until everyone is included. Anytime a player calls out "Lima beans!" the action changes to fast motion, or back to slow motion.

▶ When you play "Hug Tag," the only time you're safe from being tagged is when you're hugging another player. (This game is great fun for parents and small children and has been known to get not-too-friendly siblings to hug and like it.)

▶ "All on One Side" is a volleyball game with four or five players on one side, none on the other, and a balloon for a ball. The object is to get your team to the other side of the net and back as many times as possible. Each player volleys the balloon to another player, then scoots under the net. The last player to touch the balloon taps it over the net and scoots under. The receiving players try to keep the balloon in play and repeat the process. Later, try putting two balloons into play at one time.

In another version, which begins with players on both sides, a player who hits the ball over the net moves immediately to the other side. Everyone wins when the teams have switched sides completely without dropping the ball.

▶ "Reverse Score" can be played with various sports. Every time you score on the other team, they get a point. Then the players who score switch immediately to the "winning" team, which is the team with the most points, but which won its points by being scored upon. (My family tried this with soccer at an eighth birthday party, with very amusing results.)

▶ "Double-Up Musical Chairs" can be played by any number of children. Start with one chair less than the number of children playing. When the music stops, someone has to double up on one chair. For the next round, remove another chair for more doubling up. By the last round, everyone piles on the same chair (and on top of each other, of course). No one is left out.

▶ For "Human Knot," ten or twenty people gather closely together in a circle. Each person grabs a hand of two different people who aren't right next to him or her. The idea is to undo all of that without releasing handholds. (You twist and turn and put your arms over your shoulders.)

CREATIVE GAME-CHANGING

When two people of unequal ability — parent and child, older sibling and younger — play skill games, the one who always loses feels frustrated. The better player doesn't have much fun either, since there's no challenge when you expect to win all the time. And sometimes both winner and loser simply tire of the same old game.

You can change the rules of the games you play to meet the needs of the players. Flexibility and creativity are the key words. As long as both players agree, anything goes (except making mistakes or losing on purpose, since children see through those ploys).

Here are several suggestions for creative game-changing that will even the odds in many games and sports. They include handicapping, re-taking moves, and other special privileges that make playing more enjoyable for everyone.

CHECKERS AND CHESS

▸ Play one game as a "test game." The winner counts how many checkers are left on the board, then starts the second game with that many fewer than the normal number.

Example: If the winner ends up with five checkers on the board, next time he starts with only seven instead of the usual twelve. Continue this in subsequent games.

▸ Give the weaker player several free moves at the start of the game. Or, in checkers, give her more kings to begin with. Or declare her the winner if she gets a single king or three kings.

▸ If your child knows strategy, try this: If she can tell you a good move to make, you can't make that move.

▸ Eliminate competition altogether by having both players talk over each move, seeking and agreeing on the best ones.

OTHER BOARD GAMES

▸ For games like Sorry!, send the less adept player's piece back only ten spaces instead of all the way home. Or switch sides halfway through.

▸ When playing Monopoly, the weaker player can receive $400 instead of $200 when landing on GO. If one player goes bankrupt, keep playing anyway for a predetermined length of time.

▸ In racing board games like Candyland, set a timer for five minutes. Take turns drawing cards, and either one of the players can take the move, depending on who it helps the most (or hurts the least). The game is won if both players get across the finish line before the buzzer goes off.

▸ When playing Scrabble or similar word games, look up words before placing them on the board. (This also serves to emphasize learning.)

▸ To make Chinese checkers a cooperative game, players coordinate their marbles' movements so they reach their destinations as close to simultaneously as possible.

BOWLING

▶ To even things up and make the game more fun for you and your child, try bowling each frame together. The weaker player rolls the first ball, and the better bowler tries to "clean up."

▶ Use the official system of handicapping in bowling: Play the first game, then subtract the lesser score from the greater one. Give the weaker player 75 percent of the difference with which to start the next game.

▶ Have each bowler compete against himself, with the winner being the player who improves his own score the most from one game to the next.

CARD GAMES

▶ Play a game of solitaire together, alternating turns playing the cards. If the game "comes out," you're both winners.

▶ For five-card poker, let your child exchange four or all five cards but limit yourself to one or two. Or let her exchange one card at a time, up to five, so she can build the best possible hand.

PING-PONG AND TENNIS

▶ Set higher winning point totals for better players, lower for less experienced ones.
   Example: The better player has to make 21 points to win, but the less experienced player needs only 14.

▶ Play one game as a "test game." Subtract the weaker player's score from the stronger player's score. For the next game, the stronger player must play the difference with her "wrong" hand.
   Example: The stronger player gets 14 points, the weaker player gets 10 points. For the next game, the stronger player must play 4 points with her "wrong" hand.

▶ For ping-pong: Draw a box on the floor with chalk and confine the better player to it.

▶ For tennis: Require the stronger player to hit all balls into the white-outlined box used for serving. Or make it a rule that the better player has to let the ball bounce on his side before hitting it — no running up to the net.

▶ Forget about keeping score and try to volley for as long as you can. Keep count or have someone time you with a stop watch. Try to beat your record for the previous game.

TEAM SPORTS

▶ Relax rigid rules so no officials are needed, and let anyone participate. Allow free substitution at any time. Consider dispensing with scoring altogether.

    Example: When playing volleyball, the two teams play until the agreed-upon time expires. Try unlimited hits on each side.

▶ Change the scoring in basketball so the stronger players get 2 points for a ball in, while the younger or weaker players get 4 points for a ball in, 3 points if it hits the rim, and 2 points if it hits the backboard.

▶ In one version of basketball, each player receives the usual points for a ball through the hoop, minus one-fifth of the number of points scored by the other team while the player is in the game. This makes the combined score of the teams zero while maintaining an incentive to play defense.

BILLIARDS

▶ For eight ball, play a "test game" first and count how many balls the less experienced player has left when the game is over. The stronger player starts the next game with that many extra balls.

▶ Another creative change is to require the more able player to bank every other ball.

▶ Other interesting possibilities: Have the better player switch hands (righties play with the left hand) or wear an eye patch to decrease depth perception.

▶ For cooperative billiards, one player shoots until he misses a shot, and then it's the next person's turn. Players try to set up the next person for a good shot.

FRISBEE

▶ Before play begins, players state which hand they will use for throwing and which for catching (or the same hand for both). They stand 15–20 yards apart and take turns tossing the Frisbee or similar throwing toy.

If the catcher can't possibly reach the Frisbee at any time during its flight, the catcher gets a point. If she might have caught it, the thrower gets a point (the catcher is the one who decides). Two points are awarded to the thrower if the catcher touches the Frisbee but drops it. Two points also go to the thrower if the catcher uses the wrong hand or catches it against the body.

Play to 11 or 21 points, switching sides when one player reaches 6 or 11 points.

BODY-BRAIN WORKOUTS

Here are more ways to enhance ordinary physical activities so they exercise the brain, not just the body.

▶ Combine sports creatively. If unicycling isn't challenging enough, try juggling while doing it. Try shooting baskets from a unicycle. Experiment with combinations of volleyball and baseball.

▶ Play almost any ball game using water balloons.

▶ If you have a home video game system, try manipulating the joystick with your toes.

▶ Find out how different animals get around, then imitate their movements.

Example: Your young child hops around the room like a cricket while you provide a staccato beat on a drum (or a cake pan) for him to follow.

- Try flying a kite by attaching a helium balloon to it. (Stay clear of power lines!)

- When playing basketball, the player who has just made a basket has to answer a question before the point is counted. Decide in advance what type of questions to use: trivia, personal, outlandish, or whatever.

- Check into folk dancing opportunities for families in your community. Not only does folk dancing burn up lots of calories, but it's also a good way to learn about other cultures.

■ ■

WEIRD SPORTS

In recent years, several unusual sports have been invented and enjoyed by hardy aficionados. See if your child can add to this list by collecting magazine articles about actual sports.

- "Skijaks" are 11-foot-long polyethylene pontoons that are a cross between skis and kayaks. You use them to propel yourself across the surface of water with an oversize, twin-bladed paddle.

▶ In white-water ballooning, you take off into the sky, then descend into rapids along with your balloon.

▶ For "snow boarding," you use arm balance and hip-turning motions, like a surfer or a skate boarder, as you ride a "snow board" almost five feet long down a snowy hill.

▶ "Landsailing" boats, with wheels for sailing on dry land and a chassis that envelops the pilot, were first made of scrap wood in 1931. Others were later converted from ice boats. Today their colorful sails are made of Dacron and Mylar.

▶ "Paraskiing" is the art of skiing uphill. Wearing a parachute, you're lifted by a gust of wind and carried toward the top of the mountain. Then you touch down on the snow with your skis and proceed down the mountain. Ski-chutes are designed for the unpredictable winds of Alpine slopes and controlled by special vents that respond to a steering bar.

▶ "Wallyball," a cross between volleyball and racquetball, uses a slightly smaller, softer, rubber-textured ball. Players in teams of two, three, or four serve over a net eight feet high stretched across a racquetball court. They are allowed to hit the ball off one wall per hit. If the ball hits two walls or if it hits the opponent's back wall, a point goes to the other team.

Other weird sports are played only in people's imaginations. Here's one example; see if your child can make up some more.

▶ Under the heading "Silly Sports," *The Atlantic Monthly* in March, 1988 ran a short piece describing "Sky-Driving": Competitors drive autos out of a cargo plane at 10,000 feet and vie for a single empty parking space at a shopping mall. (Parachutes are packed in the trunk for safety, the article wryly adds.)

And let's not forget the strange and silly things people do to get into the record books. For example:

▶ Fifteen-year-old Michael Kettman of Florida won a spot in the 1989 *Guinness Book of World Records* by spinning ten basketballs on his body for five seconds. He spent countless hours perfecting his technique. His equipment included some

skateboard knee pads with attached metal rods on his legs, and two wood contraptions for spinning balls on his head and stomach.

Your child might enjoy inventing outrageous physical stunts.

▶ Encourage your child to keep records on her performance behavior and improvement (pounds lifted, sit-ups completed, and so on). These can take the form of computerized listings or graphs, or be recorded in a personal feelings diary (see pages 17-19).

▶ Play a variation of the game "H-O-R-S-E," in which players take turns attempting various shots at a basketball hoop. When one player makes a shot, the next one must make the same shot or take a letter ("H," "O," and so on) as a penalty. A player is out of the game when she completes a whole word.

Take turns choosing difficult or amusing words to use in competition.

▶ Your child may have played or watched a sport in which the umpire or coach uses hand signals to indicate a variety of meanings. Suggest that he make up a new set of signals for a homemade or existing game.

■ ■

▶ Riding a stationary bicycle is a fine way for everyone to stay in shape, but it can quickly get boring. In my experience, reading while you cycle can renew your enthusiasm. Help your child find the right light-reading "exercise bike books" or magazines to hold her interest during the exercise period.

▶ Discuss with your child the importance of positive thinking on athletic performance. Some sports psychologists believe that the difference between two athletes who have neared the top of their sport is four-fifths mental. That is, athletes may be nearly identical in their physical conditioning, but their mental attitudes will decide who wins.

What are some ways you and your child can test this theory?

> An obvious adjunct to any recreational interest is a related magazine subscription. Specialty magazines exist in vast numbers, and in fact, simply perusing the shelves at a well-stocked bookstore or library may suggest a whole new interest to your child.

TEN WAYS TO MAKE WALKING INTERESTING AGAIN

Walking is one of the best physical activities for getting and staying in shape for a lifetime. Like stationary bicycling, however, it can get dull if all you do every day is take the same old walk. Here are ways to make it more appealing. Brainstorm others with your child.

1. Change the time of day you normally walk.
   Examples: Go for a moonlight walk, or head out early in the morning before anyone else is up.

2. Take a bird-watching walk or a nature walk. Hunt for pine cones and dried pods to use later for crafts or table centerpieces. Look for animal tracks (even in the city).

3. Go on a "what's wrong" walk. Point out things around the neighborhood that need fixing or changing.
   Examples: A lawn needs mowing, a house needs painting, weeds need pulling, a sidewalk needs repair, trash needs picking up, a fence needs fixing, a roof is missing shingles, roses need pruning.
   Or take a "what's right" walk, searching out pleasing images and scenes. This increases your child's powers of observation and sense of aesthetics.

4. Try a "never-seen-before" walk. As you travel an overly familiar route, look for ten things you've never noticed before, from the way potted plants are arranged on someone's front porch to cracks in the street that remind you of a cracked eggshell.

5. Right after a rainstorm, take a "puddle walk." Notice differences in puddle sizes and make predictions about which

will dry up first. Measure their depth with a stick. Go back the next day and check on your predictions.

6. Rate the houses you pass on your walk, and give each one a grade based on predetermined criteria: ugliness (or attractiveness) of color, loudness (or absence) of barking dogs, amount of unraked (or neatly piled) leaves.

7. Play "Who Lives Here?" Try to guess what each homeowner does for a living. Use clues such as the car in the driveway and whatever you can see through the windows (without staring too much).

8. Count the cats. You have to look sharply, as they have a habit of walking softly, blending in, and relaxing in odd places, such as roofs and porch niches.

9. Plan a neighborhood picnic. Pack a lunch, walk a decent distance (until you're reasonably winded), then sit on a curb somewhere and eat.

10. Drive to a different neighborhood nearby and bring a map along. Walk randomly for half an hour, trying to get lost, then take out the map and find your way back to the car.

SPORTS SCIENCE

Another way to enliven your child's interest in physical activity is to explore the scientific side of sports. This offers other specific benefits as well. The child who analyzes a sport and understands something of its physics can incorporate this knowledge into his own movements for improved performance. And even a rudimentary knowledge of gravity, acceleration, kinetic and potential energy, and momentum will come in handy when these topics are studied later in physics class.

Increased awareness also adds a new dimension to spectator sports. You see the action differently once you know that a batter has less than 0.2 second to decide whether to swing at a 90 mph pitch, and that starting a swing 3 milliseconds too soon or too late will result in a miss. (Information from *SportScience;* see Resources, page 99.)

▶ Peter J. Brancazio, a physics professor at Brooklyn College and an amateur basketball player, analyzed the trajectories of seventy-seven basketball shots to come up with this winning formula:

— A high-arching shot is more likely to fall in the basket. (Brancazio found that all the best shooters favor the rainbow parabola over the line drive.)

— The slower the ball is delivered from the hand, and the more feathery its flight, the better the odds are that the shot will drop through the hoop. (Brancazio concluded that shooters should exert the least possible launching force.)

Ask your child to try these techniques for herself and evaluate the results.

▶ If your child has tired of plain kite flying with the common diamond kite, he may get excited by a stunt kite, which requires coordinating two strings and a lot of active involvement.

It's also fun to build a kite from a kit. Look for inexpensive kits in stores that specialize in kites or creative toys. Or your child can make a kite entirely from scratch using plastic sheeting and 1/8" dowels.

▶ Older children can design games requiring different amounts of effort. To check on how much energy is expended, they can measure one another's heart rate, respiration, and perspiration.

▶ Ask your child to try adapting common games so physically challenged children could play them.

Examples: How would you change a relay race or a tennis game if your partner was in a wheelchair? How could two people with limited arm power play volleyball?

▶ Because extended periods of weightlessness cause bone loss, scientists are researching new ways for astronauts to exercise during long space fights. Ask your child to work on solutions to this problem.

Examples: How could you compress a thorough workout into a short period of time so it wouldn't interfere with the demands of the space mission? How could astronauts run? (One possibility: Elastic cords could be used to keep a

runner on the "ground" and provide resistance.) What about weight lifting in a weightless environment? (Scientists are considering artificial gravity.)

▶ How would you play Earth games on the moon? Since the moon's gravity is one-sixth that of Earth, a football field would have to be six times as large, because players could throw the ball that much farther.

Can your child come up with ways to adapt other common games? What about for play on planets with stronger gravity?

▶ Modern technology has revolutionized sports, and who knows what the future holds? Perhaps your child can venture some creative guesses.

Just as an example of what improving technology can do: In track and field, using wooden poles, athletes have improved their pole-vaulting performance over the years from a height of around eleven feet in 1900 to just under fifteen feet in 1950. After the fiberglass pole was introduced, vaulters quickly achieved heights of more than sixteen feet. Today's records are several feet higher.

With your child, investigate how world sports records have evolved over the last few decades, and make predictions of what these records may be ten or twenty years from now. Your child can write down these predictions and seal them in an envelope to be opened in the future.

RESOURCES

American Sports Poems selected by R. R. Knudson and May Swenson (Orchard/Franklin Watts, 1988). An offbeat mix of poems on every sport from archery and auto racing to fencing, polo, and wrestling. It includes verses by such masters as Elizabeth Bishop, Anne Sexton, Randall Jarrell, Robinson Jeffers, James Merrill, and John Berryman.

Animal Town Game Co., P.O. Box 2002, Santa Barbara, California 93120. Request a catalog from this designer and distributor of cooperative and non-competitive board games. They also sell educational books and toys not readily available elsewhere, including *The New Games Book* edited by Andrew Fluegelman (Doubleday, 1976).

Blood and Guts: A Working Guide to Your Own Insides by Linda Allison (Little, Brown & Co., 1976). Absorbing activities for increasing awareness of how the body works, with many sports connections (for example, comparisons of average resting pulse rates for different types of athletes).

The Cooperative Sports & Games Book and *The Second Cooperative Sports and Games Book* by Terry Orlick (Pantheon, 1978 and 1982, respectively). Hundreds of games for children and adults that provide challenge without competition. Many are from other cultures.

Everybody's a Winner: A Kid's Guide to New Sports and Fitness by Tom Schneider (Little, Brown & Co., 1976). With sections on testing your endurance, t'ai chi ch'uan, homemade sports equipment, and how to relax.

Everybody Wins: 393 Non-Competitive Games for Young Children by Jeffrey Sobel (Walker and Company, 1983). Games for ages 3–10, most compiled from other books, some using ideas combined from more than one author. All are based on the author's experience as a recreation counselor.

The Family Fitness Handbook by Bob Glover and Jack Shepherd (Penguin Books, 1989). A multitude of ways for parents to motivate their kids toward a healthier way of life, including sections on imaginative fitness workouts and games.

Family Pastimes, RR 4, Perth, Ontario, Canada K7H 3C6. Request a catalog from this company, whose motto is "Play together, not against each other." You'll find board games, group games, and sports and games manuals.

Guinness Sports Record Book (Sterling, published annually). This comprehensive sports reference book might lead the thoughtful young sports enthusiast in many creative directions. It includes rule changes, game histories, and hundreds of charts and lists.

The Last Legal Spitfire and Other Little-Known Facts about Sports by Barbara Seuling (Doubleday, 1975). Fun tidbits, like the fact that the word "love," which means "no score" in tennis, comes from the French l'oeuf, which means "egg."

Newton at the Bat: The Science in Sports edited by Eric W. Schrier and William F. Allman (Charles Scribner's Sons, 1984). This book is a compilation of sports columns that appeared in the magazine *Science 84*. It examines the role of physics, physiology, aerodynamics, and technology in baseball, basketball, tennis, sailing, bowling, weight lifting, bicycling, and other sports. Readers learn the physics of Frisbees, the limits of human endurance, and what makes a curve ball curve and a boomerang return.

Playfair: Everybody's Guide to Noncompetitive Play by Matt Winstein and Joel Goodman (Impact Publishers, 1980). For all ages. Lots of fun games clearly described.

Sharing the Joy of Nature: Nature Activities for All Ages by Joseph Cornell (Dawn Publications, 1989). This warm, imaginative, family activity book includes suggestions for a barefoot walk, a blindfolded walk, and many other ways to increase children's awareness of the natural world.

SportScience by Peter J. Brancazio (Simon and Schuster, 1983). Written by a physicist and sports fan, SportScience explains the scientific principles behind many sports and how to apply them to improve athletic performance. Although this book is complex, older youngsters might enjoy dipping into the sections related to their current sports interests.

Sports Illustrated for Kids. This monthly magazine, available on newsstands or by subscription, includes news tidbits on all aspects of sports, articles about kids and adults who excel in sports, ideas for games, and a poster in each issue. Write: Sports Illustrated for Kids, P.O. Box 830606, Birmingham, Alabama 35282-9487; toll-free telephone 1-800-632-1300.

Sportworks by the Ontario Science Centre (Addison-Wesley, 1989). More than 50 games and activities explore the science of sports, including how to calculate a heartbeat, why your hands sweat, the science of landing gently, making a helmet for an egg, and locating the sweet spot on a baseball bat.

Super Flyers by Neil Francis (Addison-Wesley, 1988). How to make paper gliders, helicopters, parachutes, kites, and other flying toys.

The World's Best Sports Riddles & Jokes by Joseph Rosenbloom (Sterling, 1988). For ages 6–11. A collection of riddles and jokes about every sport, illustrated with cartoon athletes. Indexed.

World Wide Games, Colchester, Connecticut 06415; toll-free telephone 1-800-243-9232. Request a catalog from this distributor of handcrafted games, many from different countries and cultures. Includes a section on kites.

CHAPTER 8

Dirt, Worms, Bugs, and Mud: Kids in the Garden

When you introduce your children to an empty plot of earth and tell them it's theirs to garden, all they see at first is a large, dark-colored sandbox just waiting for them to dig in and mess around.

There's nothing wrong with that. Once children are in school, they rarely have the chance to work with messy substances. Gardening gives them ample opportunities to play in the dirt — digging holes and handling soil, peat moss, worms, water, even compost. Luckily, these are all vital to the process of coaxing nature to produce.

Children who garden grow in many ways. As they're taught to respect and cooperate with the natural world, they learn patience, how to plan, how to follow directions, and how to observe results. They develop an awareness of natural cycles. Their interest in nutrition and their feelings of self-reliance

increase when the things they plant become things they can eat and share with their family and friends.

Gardening is also an art. Combining various forms, sizes, and colors of plants into an attractive whole — creating living beauty — takes a good eye as well as a green thumb. The visually aware child will appreciate the aesthetics of growing flowers; the less aware child's aesthetic sense can be developed by the parent who points out what to look for. Creativity blossoms as the child discovers that most of the "rules" of gardening are flexible and open to experimentation.

Psychological benefits include the joy of nurturing living things and seeing them develop, and the responsibility of caring for something over a period of time. Gardening can be highly therapeutic for people of all ages, as it provides respite from more structured and competitive endeavors. And it makes an outstanding long-term family project.

"Gardens teach patience and gardens teach process," says Richard Stretz, a gardening writer, educator, and hybridizer of day lilies. "Those are not always lessons kids want to learn. But once you get them hooked, they'll be gardeners for life."

CHOOSING WHERE AND WHAT TO PLANT

Almost any home can support some kind of garden. Once you determine the best place for yours — in the back yard, on a porch, or in containers inside or outside — you and your child can start researching and planning what to grow.

The Resources section on pages 117-120 offers numerous starting points for investigation, as do the gardening sections of bookstores and the library. Send for seed catalogs and study them. What kinds of plants grow in your area, and how sturdy and disease-resistant are they? What time of year should you start them? Visit local nurseries for advice on what's appropriate for beginners in your part of the country. For speedier and more certain results, plant seedlings instead of seeds, though your child will miss out on the excitement of that first sprout peeking through the soil.

"Children like quick results," Richard Stretz advises. His experiences in gardening with children have taught him that

simple, quick-growing vegetables are good choices for turning young people on to the pleasures of gardening.

Vegetables can be grown in a small area and are highly rewarding. Carrots and radishes are good for novices, as they grow fairly quickly and can be eaten raw. In fact, all vegetables taste especially good when eaten fresh from the garden, and children who grow their own tend to enjoy vegetables more than the average child.

Container gardening offers distinct advantages: You can choose and control the soil and the drainage and avoid most garden pests. Vegetables that can be grown in larger containers (three- to five-gallon pots) include beans, carrots, peppers, tomatoes, corn, broccoli, cabbage, kale, leeks, even melons. Smaller containers (all the way down to four- to six-inch pots) are fine for growing vining peas, lettuce, spinach, and Swiss chard. Choose in-between sizes for beets, eggplants, and cherry tomatoes. Tips: Successful container gardening requires full sun and abundant water. The smaller the container, the less tolerant the plants are of drying out.

Flowers come in an amazing array of forms and colors. The seeds themselves are available in stunning variety. Some, like begonia seeds, are as small as dust and can be sneezed away, while others, like the coconut, are large enough to knock you out. Although the most common flowers are generally the least expensive and the easiest to grow, rarer types provide a special thrill to the diligent youngster. Annuals are fast, but perennials last and last. Try a little of each — annuals, perennials, and vegetables — for the child who hates being confined to one thing at a time.

Kids also like plants that appeal to many senses: fragrant mint, scented geraniums that smell like nutmeg, lemon, rose, or menthol. Ornamental popcorn is an especially delightful outdoor plant with a bonus — the kernels can be harvested and popped. Giant sunflowers add drama to any garden.

Other easy and attractive plants to grow include flowering maple, impatiens, Moses-in-the-bulrushes, piggyback plant, and strawberry begonia.

Anaheim chili PEPPER

MEDIUM HOT

ADVANCE PLANNING

When starting out, think small. Garden chores can quickly become overwhelming for the child who over-plants.

Get your child real garden tools and teach him to use and care for them responsibly. Consider buying a watering can — easier for the small child to manage than a hose (though hoses are more fun). If your child will be using a hose, it should have an adjustable nozzle with a fine spray.

Have your child draw a map of the proposed garden, showing where each plant will be placed. Tips: If you're planting sunflowers or Indian corn, put them on the north side of the garden, so when they grow up tall, they won't block sunshine from reaching the other plants.

Let your child decide how to mark what's planted — with pens on Popsicle sticks, empty seed packets attached to sticks, writing or drawing on the plastic markers sold at nurseries, or whatever.

Help your child plan some walkways so she'll be able to reach all parts of the garden to care for the plants. Lay bricks or flagstones in the soil, or line the walkways with pebbles and cover them with wood chips.

Preparing the soil is critical. For a five-by-five-foot garden, work a large sack of peat moss and one of air-dried cow's manure into the top eight inches of soil. For potted plants, add some peat moss to a packaged soil mixture.

■ ■ ■ ■ ■ ■ ■ ■ ■ ■ ■ ■ ■ ■ ■ ■ ■ ■ ■

A RECIPE FOR HOMEMADE COMPOST

If your soil needs more help than moss and manure can give it, you may want to make your own compost. This takes about six weeks, so plan ahead. Follow these simple (if smelly) steps:

1. Start with a garbage can's worth of grass clippings or leaves. Spread half on the ground and cover with an inch of soil.

2. Add a layer of bone or blood meal.

3. Now add a layer of manure equal to the amount of clippings.

4. Follow with more layers of the same items (clippings, meal, manure), then cover with a thin layer of soil.

5. Spread wastes from your kitchen on top of this.

6. Sprinkle the pile with water, and turn it all over once a week.

Eventually, microbial action will decay the whole organic mess so you can add it to the soil in your garden.

If you can tolerate the odor, you can concoct a smaller, simpler version of compost by letting a five-gallon pail of leaves and soil molder away in a warm corner of a balcony or porch. Stir it up every week and keep it moist. Or put your "ingredients" into a large trash bag, tie it, and shake it every so often.

Other common (and odor-free) household wastes you can add directly to the soil in your garden or flower pots are coffee grounds, peanut or sunflower shells, tea, and crushed eggshells.

■ ■ ■ ■ ■ ■ ■ ■ ■ ■ ■ ■ ■ ■ ■ ■ ■ ■ ■

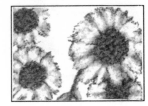

PLAYING IT SAFE

Keep gardening fun by teaching your child these four basic safety rules:

1. Always wear gloves when working with tools or rough materials.

2. Always wear sunscreen when working outdoors.

3. Stay away from all garden poisons, including pesticides and chemical fertilizers. (If you as an adult choose to use these products, then you should be the one who handles and applies them.)

4. To avoid itchy discomfort later, always wash or shower after rummaging among plants or weeds.

LEARNING IN THE GARDEN

▶ Gardens can stand some neglect before perishing. Still, the best results, as your child will soon discover, come from paying attention to each plant's individual needs.

He'll learn that plants generally like to be watered deeply only when they dry out (too much water kills more plants than not enough). Weeding is necessary not only for aesthetic reasons but because weeds crowd the plants' roots and steal their nutrients. Rows of seedlings need to be thinned as soon as they begin to get crowded. Sometimes the tiny thinned-out seedlings can be transplanted — worth a try if the thought of tossing them is traumatic.

▶ Answer your child's questions and ask some of your own. Have a couple of reference books on hand for the hard ones, like: Why do bees visit flowers? Why do you have to water and how do you know when? Why do flowers bloom at different times? Why don't many plants bloom in the winter?

▶ How about planting an "Old Smoothie," the only modern thornless rose? It's available at nurseries or by mail order.

Take this opportunity to discuss why a thornless rose is so rare, and how numerous plants and flowers have ways to protect themselves against their enemies.

▶ It's fun to grow a flowering bulb indoors (though many are toxic, so supervise younger gardeners). First, cut a bulb in half to show your child the tiny embryo (plant) surrounded by fleshy layers of scales (food). Point out that the part of an onion we eat is really a bulb.

The process of making bulbs bloom indoors is called "forcing," and you'll need to buy bulbs especially prepared for this purpose. These usually go on sale in late summer through late fall.

An easy bulb to force is the sweet-smelling Tazetta narcissus, or paperwhite narcissus. Start by planting three or four bulbs in light potting soil, sand, or small pebbles, in a pot without drainage holes. Cover them halfway, with their points sticking out (other types of bulbs should be fully covered by the planting medium; check the directions if you choose something besides paperwhites). Water and keep in a cool, dark place for ten days. Once the roots have anchored and the shoots are three inches high, move the pot to a cool, sunny window. Water regularly, keeping the roots wet. Expect flowers in about four weeks.

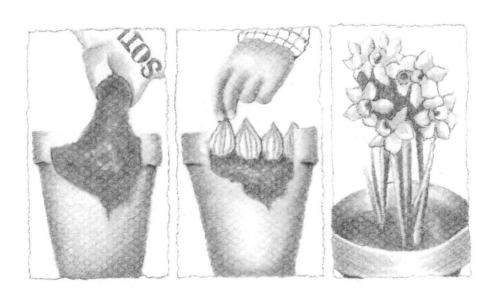

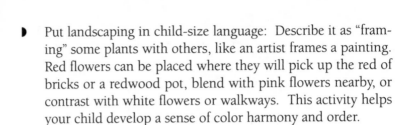

▶ Put landscaping in child-size language: Describe it as "framing" some plants with others, like an artist frames a painting. Red flowers can be placed where they will pick up the red of bricks or a redwood pot, blend with pink flowers nearby, or contrast with white flowers or walkways. This activity helps your child develop a sense of color harmony and order.

▶ Children often want to plant seeds left over from edible fruits (peach pits, apple seeds, watermelon seeds). If your local climate is conducive, try planting some peach pits in a corner of the back yard. Within about three years, some tasty fruit may appear.

Apples are another story. It can take up to twelve years for an apple tree to bear fruit, and even then, the odds are one in 50,000 that it will taste good. Home-grown apple seedlings tend to be randomly cross-pollinated with crab apples. That's why fruit trees sold by nurseries are produced by grafting buds from known varieties onto root stock.

For other seeds, it never hurts to plant them and wait to see what happens.

Eat the Fruit, Plant the Seed contains many details on growing other fruit seeds that make interesting plants (avocado, oranges, pomegranates, and more). See Resources, page 118.

▶ It's inevitable that pests will try to stake their claim to your child's garden. Together, research options for dealing with bugs and seek alternatives to poisonous chemicals. Discuss the balance of nature, how each predator has prey, and how some insects — ladybugs, for instance — are good for the garden (they eat aphids that devour roses). Other invaders aren't a problem at all; worms, for example, aerate the soil and are great to have around. Some flying bugs pollinate other plants. (Perhaps a discussion of "the birds and the bees" is suitable here?)

▶ Make scarecrows to discourage pesky birds. An old shirt on a contraption of crossed sticks is a place to start. Add pants stuffed with newspaper or straw.

Another way to scare birds away is by tying foil pie plates or long, thin strips of aluminum to a nearby fence or tree.

▶ How about collecting and studying insects? Even weeds lend themselves to collecting and arranging into weed bouquets.

▶ Discuss how different plants have been used throughout history to cure and to kill.

    If you're in the San Diego, California area, visit the Sinister Garden at Kaiser Permanente Hospital (4647 Zion Avenue, San Diego). There are actually two parts to this unusual garden. The first contains toxic plants such as poinsettia, elephant ear, hydrangea, ensata iris, oleander, and philodendron. Eating any part of these plants can be deadly. The seeds or berries of wisteria, lantana, bird of paradise, and holly are also poisonous. The second part of the garden features apothecary plants. These are plants with a medicinal purpose, such as foxglove, from which we get the heart stimulant digitalis, and periwinkle, which is used in cancer chemotherapy. Brochures are available at the front desk.

■ ■ ■ ■ ■ ■ ■ ■ ■ ■ ■ ■ ■ ■ ■ ■ ■ ■ ■ ■

THE GARDEN JOURNAL

Suggest that your child keep a garden notebook or journal. Like any diary, this is a good writing exercise. In this case, it's also a useful record of gardening events, decisions, mistakes, and successes that your child can turn to from one year to the next.

A loose-leaf binder works well for this purpose, since it allows for pages to be arranged and rearranged. Otherwise, any notebook or scrapbook will do.

▶ Things to keep track of include when specific seeds were planted, when they were fertilized, how long they took to sprout, and (for vegetables) when they were harvested.

▶ Have your child record sizes and colors of finished specimens. Measure cabbages and sunflowers; count cherry tomatoes. Chart a particular plant's growth over the weeks.

▶ A garden journal is the perfect place to make plans. Near each plant's name or picture (perhaps cut from a seed catalog), your child can write down facts about when to thin and when to transplant, how long it takes to grow, and so on.

- Encourage your child to personalize her garden journal by drawing the garden and individual plants, writing her thoughts about gardening, and so on. Include "before" and "after" photographs. If you order seeds from a catalog, cut out the catalog pictures, tape or paste them in the journal, and record important dates: planting, first sprout, first bud or flower. Over time, the journal becomes a kind of "baby book" for your child's growing plants.

- Here's a deceptively simple "assignment" for your child to include in a garden journal: Have him choose one flower and examine it very closely while describing in words exactly what he sees.

   Help out with some suggestions: "Notice the way the light and shadows connect...Look deep inside the flower...Examine the petals, the stem, the leaves..." Most of us are accustomed to glancing and commenting on nature — "That's such a lovely rose" — but we rarely take the time to really see. For the older child, such a description can become quite lengthy.

■ ■ ■ ■ ■ ■ ■ ■ ■ ■ ■ ■ ■ ■ ■ ■ ■ ■ ■

EXPERIMENTS FOR BUDDING GARDENERS

- When scientists do experiments, they start by proposing a problem to be investigated. A garden offers many opportunities to let your child experience this process.

   Example: Your child intends to plant a bean seed in a cup. Together, plan as many variations as possible and come up with related questions. Some ideas to try:

   (a) Water the bean in one cup twice a day (measure the amount of water), the bean in a second cup once a day, and the bean in a third cup once a week. What's the best amount of water for optimum growth?

   (b) Fertilize the soil in one cup and not in another. Which provides better conditions for growth?

   (c) Add small drain holes to one cup and not to another. Which plant prospers more?

(d) Plant beans just below the surface, half an inch below, an inch below, and two inches below. Which works best?

(e) Point one bean up and one bean down. What difference does that make?

(f) Think of situations involving light amounts and sources (sunlight? a light bulb?), a variety of moisture sources (milk? hot water?), and fertilizing agents (liquid fertilizers? animal fertilizers?).

▶ It's fun to experiment with unusual growing media.

Examples: Expect these to get results, since they use seeds that will grow under almost any conditions:

(a) Moisten a small sponge and roll it in grass seed. Place it in a saucer of water on a window sill. Watch what happens.

(b) Line the inside of an empty half-pint glass jar with blotting paper. Fill the jar with sawdust, and place kernels of corn and bean seeds between the blotter and the glass. Water the sawdust regularly, and watch the seeds send shoots up and roots down.

(c) Put some pebbles and water in a shallow pan. Place in this a section of a potato that has an "eye" in it, and the top of a carrot. The "eye" will sprout, and the carrot top will develop a fern.

(d) Use toothpicks to suspend a sweet potato in a tall glass so only the tip is in water. The potato will send out a leafy vine.

▶ Show your child how to start a plant in water from a cutting, so she can see the roots develop.

Example: A sturdy plant like pothos is the perfect house plant for this experiment. Philodendron, coleus, and ivy are others. Cut a six-inch section from an existing plant and place in a glass of water. Roots will begin to grow in a matter of days.

▶ Rooting a cutting in a pot is easy, too.

Example: Using a sharp knife, cut a section from a side shoot of coleus, chrysanthemum, or succulent; your cut should be 1/4 inch below a leaf. Dip the cut end in water,

then in rooting hormone, and insert in damp rooting medium (a mixture of vermiculite and peat moss) in a shallow container. Or simply break off a piece of geranium, stick it in the ground, and wait for it to produce its own roots in a matter of weeks.

▶ Propagation and hybridizing are a fascinating field for the advanced gardener. Read enough about the subject to answer questions about how it's done, even if your child isn't quite ready to take it on himself.

▶ Less easy to grow, but fascinating to kids, is the Venus flytrap. This carnivorous plant has six tiny hairs on each leaf which shut like a trap when touched (usually by a fly). A fly is digested in a week; each leaf digests three flies before withering and being replaced. Pot in sphagnum moss and place in a dish of water in full sun to imitate the tropical jungle atmosphere the plant prefers.

▶ Research the particular conditions of your back yard. Start by purchasing a soil-test kit. Plan experiments and keep careful records.
  Examples: Try one or all of these:
  (a) Plant seeds in two adjoining pots filled with back yard soil. Does adding fertilizer to one make a difference?
  (b) Compare germination rates of seeds you buy and seeds you save from other plants.
  (c) Experiment with each of these variables: light, temperature, moisture, proximity to other plants.

▶ Be on the alert for other areas to investigate.
  Examples: Questions designed to pique the curious child's interest include:
  (a) Do additives (compost starters, earthworms) make compost better or faster?
  (b) Do plants thrive on music? (Studies have shown that some do, while others seem to prefer silence.)
  (c) Which nutrients should be added to the soil, and where should they be added (to the top, or dug in below)?
  (d) Can you grow plants not usually successful in your part of the country?

    (e) Do old seeds sprout?

    (f) How much money, if any, do you save by growing your own vegetables?

▸ Some plants are unexpectedly edible and may lead to creative cooking lessons when added to soups, salads, teas, and desserts.

    Examples: The following are okay to eat, and some have nutritional value: peonies, pansies, nasturtiums, dandelions, day lilies, squash flowers, elder flowers, carnations, violets, marigolds, sunflowers. Definitely not to be eaten are wisteria, holly, bird of paradise, hydrangea, oleander, poinsettia, and philodendron.

▸ Remember that the best science projects for kids are self-motivated.

    Example: My son Kevin once decided to plant some grass in a small flowerpot on the front porch. He poured a handful of grass seed into a small pot filled with commercial leaf mold and fertilizer (which is not the accepted procedure), covered the seeds with about an inch of soil (quite a bit deeper than the instructions on the box suggested), watered them, and finally covered them with a piece of plastic wrap to keep the moisture in.

    Every morning he checked on their progress, and within only three days, tiny sprouts appeared. Within two weeks, he had a full container of grass. Too full, as he noticed that the blades were crowding each other. He "mowed" them (with a pair of scissors). Altogether, the experiment lasted for about a month, until the blades turned yellow (the wrong growing medium? overcrowding? not enough sun on the covered porch?).

    At one point, Kevin took his personal "yard" to school, placed it in his locker, and enjoyed his friends' surprise.

GARDENING AND AESTHETICS

▸ Gardening literature can be interesting, even for the armchair gardener.

    Examples: For the youngest, don't forget the garden adventures of Beatrix Potter's *Peter Rabbit* or Ruth Krauss's

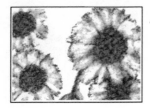

Carrot Seed; see Resources, pages 118 and 117. Older children will be amazed at how articulate gardeners have described the beauty and poetry of the natural world in a wealth of literary (not just how-to) books and articles, including Christopher Lloyd's *The Adventurous Gardener* and Eleanor Perényi's *Green Thoughts: A Writer in the Garden*; see Resources, pages 117 and 118.

▶ Add another dimension to gardening by exploring the lore and meaning of flowers.

Examples: Most of the language of flowers we're familiar with originated in the Orient and became popular in the West in Victorian times.

A flower presented in an upright position implied a positive message; upside down meant the opposite. For example, a gift of an upright rosebud meant "I fear, but I hope;" returned upside down, the message was, "Don't fear or hope."

More flowers and their meanings: carnation (fascination, woman's love); bluebell (constancy, kindness); passionflower (belief); peony (shame); rose (love, beauty).

As with all symbols, multiple meanings and interpretations are possible.

▶ Melons, squashes, and gourds can be turned into garden sculptures.

Examples: Suggest that your child carve her initials on them, then watch the letters grow bigger over time. An inventor designed plastic forms that shape eggplants, zucchini, and pumpkins into hearts, diamonds, even faces; perhaps your child can figure out a way to replicate this feat using homemade wooden forms.

▶ Carefully chosen containers can enhance the aesthetics of gardening. The handy family might enjoy constructing a window box as a project. Children can easily paint or decorate inexpensive pots. Those who enjoy crafts can make macramé plant hangers.

▶ Once cut or plucked, your child's flowers need another pleasing home, a vase of some sort. You can buy these in

splendid variety or make them out of common household materials. Encourage creativity.

▶ Make or buy a plant press to preserve plants for identifying and collecting. The simplest way is to press the plants in a very large book, but a wooden frame that allows air circulation is best.

On top of the base of the frame, put a sheet of corrugated cardboard with the corrugations running the short way. On top of this, place a sheet of blotting paper or several sheets of newspaper. Next comes the plant, folded in newspaper and labeled. Finish with more paper, another sheet of cardboard, and the top of the frame. Use rocks or books to weigh down the press. Drying time will vary.

▶ Take field trips to botanical gardens and arboretums, living proof of the myriad varieties of plant life that can be grown with knowledgeable care. Many offer brochures that explain what you're seeing and can serve as starting points for conversation.

Examples: Talk about native plants — types, characteristics, needs, and so on. (In Southern California, where I live, native plants have to be drought-resistant, and many are succulents.) This could easily turn into a discussion of the broader implications of ecology: Should we use scarce water resources to keep our lawns green? What can happen when someone introduces a non-native plant into an area where it's likely to thrive?

Some of the larger botanical gardens have "demonstration gardens," where your family may get ideas applicable to your own home garden. The gift shops in public gardens carry many unusual items related to plants and gardening, some of which may further ignite your child's interest.

▶ Visit a topiary garden. A topiary is a tree or shrub that has been clipped into a fancy, often whimsical, shape. If the idea appeals to your family, buy topiary forms from one of the mail-order horticultural supply companies. These are simply metal armatures on which vines can be trained and tied in the form of animals or whatever else you choose.

THE ART OF THE JAPANESE GARDEN

A visit to a Japanese garden will open your child's eyes to many artistic possibilities.

The traditional Japanese strolling garden is laid out with a circular path around a pond stocked with koi (small fish). The Zen ideals of simplicity and understated beauty are worked into the landscape. All of the elements, from the plants to the rocks to the water, are arranged symbolically. Rocks are usually grouped in threes, fives, or sevens, and three rocks placed on top of one another may, for example, suggest a crane. Two flat rocks on either side of a tall one represent Buddha flanked by two disciples. Water suggests purity. In some gardens, rocks, pebbles, and sand arranged in a meandering pattern suggest the effect of water. Black pines symbolize eternity.

Different interpretations are possible, so consult any brochures which are offered, or ask docents for information about symbolism.

▶ Try creating a sand garden in the Japanese tradition, said to have been started by Soseki Musoo, a fourteenth-century Kyoto philosopher. Sand gardens contain only sand, rocks, and moss, which symbolize water, mountains, and forests, respectively. The sand is raked into lines resembling lake ripples, and rocks of unusual shapes are arranged artistically, usually asymmetrically. There is a famous Japanese temple garden in which fifteen stones are placed in such a way that no matter where you stand, you can only count fourteen at a time.

For your garden, use white playbox sand. First, remove all weeds and pack the earth tightly, or put a sheet of plastic over the bed before adding the sand. Use stones, a path, or some kind of ground cover as a border for the sand garden.

As your child plans and creates his own sand garden, encourage him to develop a story, an interpretation, to go along with it.

▶ You can add a touch of Oriental design to almost any garden with Japanese lanterns, driftwood, statuary, pottery, or a small basin used as a pool.

▶ Ikebana, or flower arranging, is another Japanese gardening art, considered a form of sculpture. It relates to Eastern philosophy and centers around the beauty and peacefulness of nature. It enhances your ability to see everything around you with more sensitivity.

Oriental flower arrangers are concerned with the lines and shape of each leaf, blossom, and branch, and arrangements tend to be asymmetrical. To more accurately replicate nature, they typically use more green than flower arrangers in the West.

The artistically inclined child might enjoy learning how to do ikebana, but all children stand to benefit from some exposure to it — especially since most kids think that flower arranging means simply sticking cut flowers in a vase.

■ ■

RESOURCES

The Adventurous Gardener by Christopher Lloyd (Random House, 1983). For older children to adults. The writer-horticulturist believes "the best gardening is experimental." He makes even familiar gardening chores exciting.

Carrot Seed by Ruth Krauss (Harper & Row, 1989). A classic for preschoolers.

"A Child's Garden" is a 54-page booklet of planting projects and ideas covering many curriculum areas, with an extensive section on "getting the most from your vegetables." It includes a directory of seed companies and other resources. Write: Educational Materials, Chevron Chemical Company, Public Affairs Dept., P.O. Box 5047, Ramon, California 94583-0947.

Common Ground Garden Program, 2615 S. Grand Ave., Suite 400, Los Angeles, California 90007. Request a publications catalog. An item of special interest to parents: *Children's Gardens* by Elizabeth Brenner and John Pusey (1982). This complete "field guide for teachers, parents, and volunteers" includes educational activities and how-to's for ages 3–10.

The Complete Adventures of Peter Rabbit by Beatrix Potter (Frederick Warne, 1982). All four Potter stories featuring the mischievous rabbit.

"The Complete Guide to Gardening by Mail" lists all kinds of plants plus addresses of nurseries that offer mail-order catalogs. Write: Mailorder Association of Nurserymen, 210 Cartwright Blvd., Massapequa Park, New York 11762. Enclose a self-addressed, business-size envelope with two first-class stamps.

Eat the Fruit, Plant the Seed by Millicent E. Selsam and Jerome Wexler (William Morrow, 1980). A beginning how-to book which describes and pictures (with photos) six fruits whose seeds produce interesting plants.

"Get Ready, Get Set, GROW!" is a 15-minute video by Ian Clark, taped in and available from the Brooklyn Botanical Garden, 1000 Washington Ave., Brooklyn, New York 11225. It captures the excitement of a garden seen through the eyes of a child and includes instructive booklets for the child and parent.

Green Thoughts: A Writer in the Garden by Eleanor Perényi (Vintage/Random House, 1983). A witty collection of short essays on horticulture, by a writer sharing thirty years of amateur gardening experience. Older children may enjoy this book.

Growing Vegetable Soup by Lois Ehlert (Harcourt Brace Jovanovich, 1987). This brightly illustrated book for very young children explains how vegetables happen.

Hidden Stories in Plants by Anne Pellowski (Macmillan, 1990). The subtitle says it all: "Unusual and Easy-to-Tell Stories from Around the World Together with Creative Things to Do While Telling Them." Includes traditional tales that explain why corn has silky white hair and why trees whisper, as well as how to make a variety of crafts using natural objects.

Ikebana: Spirit and Technique by Shusui Komoda and Horst Pointner (Blandford Press/Sterling, 1980). Includes a history of ikebana and a series of lessons with photos and meanings of the various forms.

A Kid's First Book of Gardening by Derek Fell (Running Press, 1990). Packaged with a small, three-piece plastic "greenhouse" and four packets of seeds, this book offers experiments, activities, and discussions of plant needs and behavior.

Let's Grow! 72 Gardening Adventures with Children by Linda Tilgner (Storey Communications, 1988). Projects and activities for all ages. Much detail and lots of creative, unusual fun, including how to forage for wild foods, make an insect cage, and prepare apple cider.

Linnea's Windowsill Garden by Christina Bjork (Farrar, Straus & Giroux, 1988). A little girl takes five- to ten-year-olds on an amusing tour of her indoor garden, teaching them what plants need.

The Lore of Flowers by Neil Ewart (Sterling, 1982). The language of flowers, their stories and legends. Learn that one species of orchid holds almost four million seeds in a single seed capsule, and that the lily is believed to be a survivor from before the Ice Age.

National Gardening Association, 180 Flynn Avenue, Burlington, Vermont 05401. Request information about youth gardening books and resources, as well as how to locate a children's gardening project.

George W. Park Seed Co., P.O. Box 32, Greenwood, South Carolina 29640. Request a free catalog.

Peter Rabbit's Gardening Book by Sarah Garland (Frederick Warne, 1983). Peter and friends raise vegetables, berries, and flowers.

Ringer, 9959 Valley View Road, Eden Prairie, Minnesota 55344-3585; toll-free telephone 1-800-654-1047. Request a catalog from this company that sells people-safe, pet-safe natural products for lawn and garden.

Smith & Hawken, 25 Corte Madera, Mill Valley, California 94941; telephone (415) 383-2000. Request a catalog from this respected mail-order firm, which sells good quality, scaled-down versions of garden implements for children, among other gardening supplies.

Sunflowers by Cynthia Overbeck (Lerner, 1981). This book, illustrated with full-color photographs, was selected as an Outstanding Science Trade Book for Children. It provides basic facts for would-be sunflower-growers of all ages. (Did you know that sunflowers can grow to eighteen feet tall, with heads as big as two feet across?) Includes a glossary and index.

Tiger Lilies and Other Beastly Plants by Elizabeth Ring (Walker and Company, 1984). For ages 4 and up. Describes and illustrates twelve plants which have some animal characteristics, from the way they look to the way they act. Includes a glossary.

The Victory Garden Kids' Book: A Beginner's Guide to Growing Vegetables, Fruits, and Flowers by Marjorie Waters (Houghton Mifflin, 1988). Step-by-step instructions for growing a garden, including specifics for 30 crops. Illustrated with sketches and photos of real children.

Wayside Gardens, 1 Garden Lane, Hodges, South Carolina 29695-0001; toll-free telephone 1-800-845-1124. Request a free catalog listing every kind of plant and bulb.

White Flower Farms, Litchfield, Connecticut 06759-0050; toll-free telephone 1-800-888-7756. This company specializes in outdoor perennials and has a selection of gardening books. Catalogs are sold by annual subscription.

CHAPTER 9

Mind Snacks: Recipes for Kitchen Learning

I f you enjoy cooking, both you and your children are lucky, because you can naturally share with them your enthusiasm for the culinary arts. The rest of us just have to think about cooking in a different way if our youngsters are to benefit from the learning that food-related activities provide.

Kids are automatically attracted to the fun it looks like you're having when you cook. After all, you get to mess around with an infinite number of ingredients, you get to smash some of them and scrunch or pound others, you get to choose what kind of tastes you want to end up with, and you get to experiment.

The willingness and ability to experiment is the key to enjoyable and effective kitchen education. Personally, I'm a strict recipe-follower. That, too, has its pleasures for a surprising number of children, but most often the fun comes from fooling around with a variety of substances and seeing what comes out of the oven or the pot.

It helps to develop the mind-set that there's no such thing as a failure, whether the end result is edible or not. In between the fun of creating and the hoped-for delight of eating comes more learning than you can shake a steak at. For instance, your child will learn to think ahead to be sure he has the desired ingredients on hand, or suitable substitutes. Cooking also sharpens math and science skills while providing a lesson in nutrition.

If you're game to try (almost) anything your child prepares — including fried peanut-butter sandwiches — she'll be more willing to sample new foods you suggest at home and in restaurants. Encouraging your child's more inventive creations also builds self-esteem.

Even preschoolers can be involved in food preparation for themselves or the whole family. When they say "Let me do it!," let them. By school age they can carry out a multitude of adult-supervised kitchen activities, from menu planning to measuring, mixing, and actual cooking. Include cleanup chores as part of the agenda and lend a hand if your child is still young or easily overwhelmed.

At age eleven, my son Kevin was already expert at baking several kinds of chocolate-chip cookies when he tackled a triple-layer checkerboard cake made with three pans and two flavors of cake mix. The results were less than aesthetically pleasing, but he figured out a better way to bake it the next time around.

GETTING STARTED

There are many enticing cookbooks for children (see Resources, pages 133-135, for suggestions). When considering which ones to try, make sure the recipes are clear enough for your child to understand. For example, if a recipe says "sift," is that term explained? If you're a pretty basic cook yourself, like I am, your child's cookbooks will have to spell everything out. It helps to have access to a grandparent, neighbor, or friend who knows his or her way around the kitchen.

It also helps to have on hand at least one comprehensive (adult) cookbook that doesn't take anything for granted. I have referred countless times to my 1949 edition of *The Good Housekeeping Cook Book*, which my mother gave me years ago.

That's where I recently looked up how to make basic macaroni when another recipe I was using assumed I already knew that much.

Well before an actual cooking session, choose one or more recipes with your child, list together the ingredients you'll need to buy, and shop for them together. Be willing to add a little extra to your food budget for experimenting. (Think of cooking as an art or craft worth the expense, like finger painting or photography.)

Make certain you have on hand all the kitchen equipment necessary, including the right knives, mixing implements, and pans. Halfway through a recipe is no time to discover an item is missing. A nice touch for a very young child is a heat-resistant, clear glass cooking pot that allows you to see the food as it cooks.

■ ■

KITCHEN SAFETY

Keep cooking a safe family activity by following these six simple guidelines.

1. Make it a rule always to turn pot handles inward, away from the edge of the stove.

2. Teach your child how to use knives safely (and never when in a hurry).

3. Emphasize the power (and the power to harm) of blenders, electric mixers, under-the-sink waste disposers, food processors, stoves, and ovens, including microwaves. Compare these appliances to power tools such as drills and chain saws and teach your child to treat them with respect.

4. Point out that a pot or pan stays hot long after it leaves the stove. So do the burners on an electric range, long after you've turned them off.

5. Make sure that your child always wears a large apron when cooking as protection from hot splatters.

6. Have plenty of oven mitts and potholders available. Your child can practice using these on cold dishes before handling hot ones.

■ ■

OVER-THE-COUNTER LEARNING

▶ Cooking can be an artistic way to express oneself. All people, including children, enjoy putting their personalities into their culinary concoctions. Once your child knows the basics, allow him as much freedom as possible and see what happens.

▶ Point out how foods can be made to appeal to all the senses. Talk about colors and combinations, scents, and textures as well as flavors.

▶ Encourage creativity in the forms food can take.

   Examples: Pancakes can be made in any animal shape by pouring the body first, then adding legs and a head. (A friend of ours has made this a Sunday morning family ritual: His children take turns calling out types of animals, while he designs pancakes to order.) Use cookie cutters to cut out sandwiches. Add cucumber slices to the bottom of a hot dog roll, and you have a car. Create a monster by using small round dinner rolls for sandwiches, adding grapes on pretzel sticks for eyes.

▶ Allow your child to combine foods in unaccustomed ways, or to use unexpected colors. When my son Simon was small, he wondered why food never seems to be blue. So we made cupcakes using blue food coloring. His curiosity was satisfied and lightning didn't strike.

▶ Show your child how to substitute more healthful ingredients than the ones called for, or to change some aspect of a recipe for whatever reason. Sometimes the results will be edible and sometimes they won't.

I once read that the goal of cooking classes is to liberate students from cookbooks. A worthy goal for your at-home cooking school might be to free your child from the fear of failure. Learning how to fix a dish that has gone wrong can be more educational than learning how to prepare it in the first place.

▶ Make up recipes from scratch, then name them appropriately or amusingly. Or your child can invent a name, then prepare something that tastes the way the name sounds (yellow boomerangs? slippedy slides?). Or adapt literary allusions to fit foods (a muffin of one's own? the pizza not taken? my kingdom for a quesadilla?).

▶ List all of the basic dishes your family commonly eats, then brainstorm ways to change them by altering their form, by combining their ingredients in new recipes, and so on. Since you don't have to actually prepare everything mentioned, encourage the uninhibited flow of ideas. A strawberry and ham shake might work; peanut pancakes could be delicious.

▶ Explore with your child the vocabulary of cooking. "Dice" means to cut into tiny squares shaped like dice. "Mince" means to chop into very tiny pieces. "Purée" means to make food into a smooth, thick mixture, usually using a blender or food processor. "Simmer" means to cook just below the boiling point so small bubbles rise to the surface. "Sauté" means to cook food in an open pan in a small amount of oil. And so on.

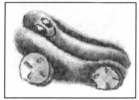

▶ Kids enjoy making their "own" items, such as individual meat loaves, cupcakes, or single-sized pizzas. Little loaf pans and baking dishes are useful at times like these.

▶ Math skills are often called on during cooking. Have a conversion chart available for when your child needs to expand a recipe to feed more than the number called for, or divide it to feed fewer. Math is also needed when a package of something doesn't come in the amount required in a particular recipe. Supply a variety of measuring utensils: a kitchen scale, multiple sets of measuring cups and spoons.

▶ Since snack foods are favorites (for some children, these provide a large part of their daily nutrition), make snack designing a priority.
Examples: For homemade Popsicles, shakes, or blender creations, stay well stocked with frozen fruit juice concentrates, cans and jars of juices, frozen fruits, fresh fruits, yogurt, milk, oats, nuts, nut butters, raisins, honey, and cinnamon.

▶ Now that elaborate salad bars are in style, take your child shopping to choose fresh ingredients and dressings for a home salad bar. Try to include at least one vegetable that neither of you has ever tasted. Turn a salad into a meal with homemade muffins.

▶ Introduce your child to the world of herbs and spices (since salt is overused and not healthful anyway). Has your child tasted parsley, sage, rosemary, and thyme?

▶ Once your child figures out that one cup of uncooked rice equals three cups of cooked rice, or that one large onion comes out to a cup of chopped onions, or that a stick of margarine is the same as half a cup, have her note these details in her recipes to save time on subsequent occasions.

▶ If your child thinks bread comes in three varieties only (the soft, white kind, the wheat kind, and hot dog buns), expand this limited repertoire.
Examples: Try Middle Eastern pita, Mexican tortillas, Scottish scones, and the breads of other lands: chapati from India, limpa from Sweden, men pau from China, and so on.

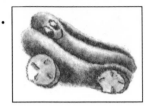

Point out that bread is extremely important as a ceremonial food. For example, in Latin America on All Souls' Day, the dead are remembered by taking bread offerings to cemeteries. *Creative Food Experiences for Children* has an interesting chapter on bread; see Resources, page 133.

FOOD TRIPS: GOING BEYOND THE KITCHEN

▶ If you have a home computer, let your child enter recipes on it. One of my sons used BASIC to work out a program of ingredient lists for our favorite recipes.

▶ Enthusiastic young cooks enjoy playing "restaurant." First, request a tour of a local fast-food eatery, or if you know someone in the restaurant business, ask for a peek behind the scenes. At home, suggest that your child make two or three kinds of cookies or other simple, popular foods, then design a menu and set up "shop." She and her friends can take turns being the restaurant manager, waitress or waiter, and customer.

▶ Teach about foreign cultures while your child learns to prepare various international dishes.

Example: Choose a country and look it up in an atlas. Write to its embassy in Washington, D.C., and request recipes for popular national dishes. (Your librarian can help you find the address.)

While you're waiting for a reply, explore the ethnic groceries in your area. Most cities have Asian food stores, Italian or Middle Eastern groceries, and Jewish delicatessens. Often such shops carry regional cookbooks with notes that can tell you a lot about the country's climate, economy, and history.

If there aren't any ethnic groceries nearby, wander the foreign foods aisle at your supermarket. Ask the grocer to explain some of the more unusual ingredients and ways they are used.

■ ■

PASTA POINTERS

There are 600 shapes and varieties of pasta, all of them easy to prepare.

Pasta is properly cooked when it's al dente, which means firm "to the tooth."

Sometimes carrots are used to color pasta orange, or spinach to make it green.

Tubes and twists are best for chunky sauces to cling to; spaghetti, linguine, and noodles are preferred for smoother sauces.

Your child might enjoy learning about and trying different types of pastas. Here are nine of the most popular:

1. spaghetti — long, round strands; from *spago,* which means "length of string" in Italian

2. lasagna — flat, wide noodles usually layered with sauce and cheese

3. conchiglie — shell-shaped macaroni; from the word meaning "seashell"

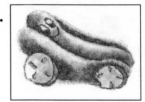

4. manicotti — large cylinders, usually stuffed with a filling; from the word meaning "small sleeves"

5. farralle — bowtie-shaped pasta; the word means "butterfly"

6. elbow macaroni — curved tubes; from *macarone,* meaning "dumpling"

7. rotelle — wheel-shaped, meaning "wagon wheel"

8. ravioli — meat- or cheese-filled squares of pasta dough

9. fusilli — curly spaghetti or macaroni, meaning "twists"

■ ■

▶ Seek out specialty food outlets such as creameries, poultry farms, perhaps even a sausage factory, any of which might make an unusual field trip.

▶ Farmers' markets are becoming more popular across the country. If you have a local farmers' market and you haven't been there yet, plan a Saturday-morning visit with your child.

   In contrast to the sterile ambience of most suburban supermarkets, the farmers' market is a noisy, bustling place. The variety of fresh foods, plants and flowers, even hand-crafted items is truly astonishing. The one I know in down-town Los Angeles is like a series of small, ethnic neighborhood markets laid end-to-end. Tip: Most stalls charge for shopping bags, European-style, so bring your own and save money.

▶ Try learning to eat with chopsticks, as the Chinese and Japanese do. Many commercially packaged chopsticks come with printed instructions. Or visit an Oriental restaurant and request a lesson.

   Once your family masters this feat, celebrate with a Japanese-style dinner. Everyone removes their shoes and sits on large, flat pillows or mats at a low table (perhaps your coffee table).

▶ Enroll your child in a local children's cooking class. Many stores that specialize in kitchen wares also offer classes. For evening

and weekend offerings, check your local community school or the community services department of your local college.

▶ Discuss what it means for a food to be "in season." Foods in season are the least expensive and often the tastiest. Different foods are in season at different times in various parts of the country. Talk about how important climate and weather are to what you find in your local supermarket.

Example: As of this writing, the prices of green peppers, tomatoes, and other vegetables are much higher than usual at my market, due to an unexpected chill that destroyed much of these crops in faraway states.

▶ Model smart shopping for your child.

Examples: Make price and quality comparisons for different food items. Buy a generic cake mix and a well-known brand. Does the taste difference justify the price difference to you? How about to your child? Figure out what it would cost to buy the ingredients to duplicate a particular fast food. Is the time savings worth the difference? Does time always equal money? What about the pleasure factor? Which seems better: to know the nutritional content of what you're eating, or to take your chances with fast food?

▶ Encourage your child to compile his own cookbook of tried-and-true recipes, perhaps illustrated with drawings or photos. Or he may prefer collecting recipes he would like to try someday. Help him to find a format that works for him.

Examples: All in a jumble in a box is what some people prefer (all right, that's what I do). Others paste favorite recipes in a loose-leaf binder, or write them on 4" x 6" or 5" x 7" cards and file them away.

As your child's personal cookbook grows, he can also ask friends and relatives for their favorite recipes.

▶ Buy a copy of a magazine devoted to cooking. A subscription might motivate your child to experiment with new recipes.

FOOD SCIENCE

▶ Help your child to make the connection between calories consumed and calories burned through exercise. Use this chart as a starting point for discussion.

One hour of exercise	Calories burned
Basketball	600
Ping-pong	360
Swimming (crawl)	480
Roller skating	420
Cycling at 10 mph	420
Walking briskly	420

▶ Talk about junk foods. What's in them, and do they make for a balanced diet? Fast foods are not normally labeled with their nutritional content, but nearly all of the big chains now offer a sheet or pamphlet of information on request. Ask or send for these so you can make comparisons. *The Fast-Food Guide* provides a detailed rundown on every aspect of this American staple; see Resources, page 134.

▶ Older children may be interested in investigating their school lunch program. Get them started with some thought-provoking questions.

Examples: Are the meals nutritionally balanced? Are they attractive? What proportion of a typical meal could be labeled junk food? Are additives used? Is there much waste? Do the teachers have the same menus as the students?

Creative Food Experiences for Children has a section on school lunches; see Resources, page 133.

▶ The next time you're at the market (and your child isn't starving), teach her how to read the labels on the canned and frozen goods you normally buy. If you don't understand everything that's printed there, send your questions to the manufacturers (be sure to include the complete name of the product) or make note of the toll-free number and call.

I once called to find out how much caffeine was in one of those gourmet low-calorie coffee-chocolate beverages. Another time, I called a vitamin company to find out exactly what "guarana" is, since that was one of the ingredients in

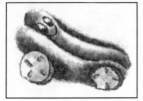

vitamin pills I was considering purchasing. (It acts like caffeine, so I decided not to give them to my children.) You might also contact the manufacturers to find out whether the carbohydrate in a cereal could be classified as a "complex carbohydrate," or how much sugar (and the ingredients that act just like sugar) is in a soft drink that claims to be "low in sugar."

▶ This simple experiment shows how chemicals from our body (the enzymes in saliva) break down starch molecules: Have your child spit into a small jar of baby food bananas or sweet potatoes. Leave the jar unrefrigerated overnight. By morning, the spit will have turned most of the starchy food into a liquid.

▶ It's easy to observe the chemistry of foods when sugar dissolves in hot water, gelatin changes from a liquid to a solid in the refrigerator, yeast causes dough to rise, water boils into steam, and a soft-boiled egg blackens a silver teaspoon (the sulfur in the egg white does it). When a child tries to stir something hot with a metal spoon, he soon understands that metal conducts heat. Next time, he'll reach for a plastic or wooden spoon.

▶ Other scientific conversation starters: Each adult consumes about half a ton of food and drink every year. The small intestine, which separates what your body can use from what it can't, is about 20 feet long in adults. The human stomach contains hydrochloric acid, which is powerful enough to dissolve cement and would burn your finger if you touched it.

■ ■

TABLE MANNERS

▶ Everyone enjoys their food more when it's served in a pleasing environment. Your child can help by making place cards to set around the table, making napkin rings, or designing a centerpiece for the table (a stuffed-animal tableau?).

▶ Talk about table manners. Discuss differences between what's acceptable at home, at a friend's house, and at a fine restaurant.

▶ Point out how manners change from one era to another, and from country to country.

Examples: In some Middle Eastern cultures, people regularly eat with their hands from a communal dish. European diners don't switch their fork back and forth from their left hand to their right when cutting and eating food, as is the custom in the United States. Instead, they keep their fork in their left hand and their knife in their right hand (unless they're left-handed, in which case it's the other way around). Try these customs at your house.

■ ■ ■ ■ ■ ■ ■ ■ ■ ■ ■ ■ ■ ■ ■ ■ ■ ■ ■ ■

RESOURCES

Babar Learns to Cook by Laurent de Brunhoff (Random House, 1978). A picture book about the amusing culinary adventures of the famous elephant family.

Cooking the Russian Way, Cooking the Thai Way, Cooking the Hungarian Way, and 19 others (Lerner Publications, 1986). For ages 10–14. This series of "easy menu ethnic cookbooks" contains clear and colorful recipes, metric conversion charts, introductions to the customs and menus of each land, and indexes. Cooking terms and special ingredients are defined.

Creative Food Experiences for Children by Mary T. Goodwin and Gerry Pollen (Center for Science in the Public Interest, 1980). For ages 3–10. With an adult's help, the activities described in this book increase children's awareness of their senses, the natural world, and their community.

Dinner's Ready, Mom: A Cookbook for Kids by Helen Gustafson (Ten Speed Press, 1986). Step-by-step guidelines so kids can prepare dinner mostly unsupervised. For youngsters old enough to manage the stove and oven safely.

Eat, Think, and Be Healthy! by Paula Klevan Zeller and Michael F. Jacobson, Ph.D. (Center for Science in the Public Interest, 1987). For ages 8–10. An adult/child activity book that teaches children how to choose healthy foods. Includes 56 multi-faceted projects.

The Fast-Food Guide by Michael Jacobson, Ph.D., and Sarah Fritschner (Workman Publishing, 1986). This book tells you everything you could possibly want to know about fast foods so you can make informed choices.

Foodworks by The Ontario Science Centre (Addison-Wesley, 1987). For ages 6 and up. More than 100 science activities and fascinating facts about food and healthy eating.

The Fun of Cooking by Jill Krementz (Knopf, 1985). Using photographs and the words of young cooks ages 6–16, the award-winning photojournalist shows readers the range of pleasurable possibilities in cooking.

Good For Me: All About Food in 32 Bites by Marilyn Burns (Little, Brown & Co., 1978). Why we eat, what happens when we do, nutrition, historical facts about food, quizzes, and activities.

Junk Food — What It Is, What It Does by Judith S. Seixas (William Morrow, 1984). A simple "read-alone book" which discusses all aspects of junk food and suggests nutritious eating habits.

Kids Are Natural Cooks: Child-Tested Recipes for Home and School Using Natural Foods prepared by the Parents' Nursery School (Houghton Mifflin, 1974). More than 60 healthful recipes for parents working with very young children. Recipes are illustrated, with every step explained carefully.

Kids Can Cook by Dorothy R. Bates (The Book Publishing Co., 1987). This spiral-bound cookbook contains vegetarian recipes kitchen-tested by 11- to 16-year-olds.

Kids Cooking: A Very Slightly Messy Manual (Klutz Press, 1987). This wire-bound volume, printed on card stock and packaged with a set of color-coded measuring spoons, contains 45 recipes for crafts and such appealing treats as Tuna Wiggle, Disgustingly Rich Brownies, and Walrus Salad.

"Kids' Kitchen" is a 23-minute video demonstrating basic cookie-baking skills to children, with lots of helpful tips. Write: Kids' Kitchen, P.O. Box 25503, Portland, Oregon 97225.

Kitchen Fun by the editors of *OWL* and *Chickadee* magazines (Little, Brown & Co., 1988). An activity book using kitchen materials. Kids learn how to turn walnut shells into magnets, make magic with a spoon, prepare edible ice puppets, and make a fish pizza. Illustrated with photographs.

Literary Gourmet: Menus from Masterpieces by Linda Wolfe (Simon & Schuster, 1989). This unusual cookbook for adults contains famous eating scenes from literature, along with recipes for the dishes served, gathered from old cookbooks. It includes recipes for hare prepared as in Horace's day, meat pies Chaucer's characters might have eaten, the *petites madeleines* of Proust's *Swann's Way*, and Southern-style biscuits mentioned in a Steinbeck short story.

The Little Pigs' First Cookbook by N. Cameron Watson (Little, Brown & Co., 1987). A picture book/storybook/recipe book in which three pig brothers share their favorite meals. With step-by-step instructions and helpful hints.

My First Cook Book by Angela Wilkes (Knopf, 1989). A "life-size guide to making fun things to eat," illustrated with full-color photographs and including lots of visually creative ways to prepare and combine simple foods.

Out to Lunch! Jokes About Food by Peter and Connie Roop (Lerner Publications, 1985). For ages 6–9. Food-related funny lines and plays on words.

Peter Rabbit's Cookery Book compiled by Anne Emerson (Viking Penguin, 1986). For ages 5–8. This collection of 21 recipes, with illustrations by Beatrix Potter, is inspired by the foods described in the *Peter Rabbit* stories.

Science Experiments You Can Eat and *More Science Experiments You Can Eat* by Vicki Cobb (Lippincott, 1972 and 1979, respectively). For ages 8–14. These are science books, not cookbooks. Readers learn how to turn a kitchen into a home laboratory. Once children master basic information about the science of food, their recipes may turn out better.

CHAPTER 10

Cultural Diversity: It's All Relative

If you and your family have traveled widely or spent time living in another country, then your children already have a strong head start on understanding what cultural relativity is all about. Otherwise, like most people of any age, they're likely to believe that the culture they're growing up in is the only "right" one and all others are a bit "funny." Most of us take for granted the givens of our own society until something makes us aware that people of other nations, religions, or ethnic backgrounds don't always experience life the way we do.

As you undertake the study of other cultures with your child, aim for an appreciation of differences. Avoid accepting or fostering cultural stereotypes. As Amy Klauke, co-editor of the multiethnic children's magazine *Skipping Stones*, puts it, "We walk a

tightrope with this kind of work [exploring cultural diversity], because we don't want to create more generalizations to replace the old ones. We hope our efforts lead children to a sense of the other as complex and mysterious, and that they will learn to allow for that difference and appreciate it." (For more information about *Skipping Stones*, see Resources, page 165.)

Especially help your child to appreciate non-Western cultures for their intrinsic worth. Ideally, an awareness of cultural diversity can also lead to an awareness of individual differences, increased appreciation of the incredible variety of human attributes, and flexible thinking. These will naturally lead to less prejudice and discrimination.

The following topics, ranging from the earthbound to the "cosmic," can be starting points for discussion. Tips: Your child will be more comfortable talking about cultural differences and stereotypes with you if you begin by admitting your own biases, fears, and ignorance. The younger the child, the more you'll want to keep the topics concrete. And whenever possible, turn your discussions into hands-on experiences.

FROM TACOS TO TOGAS: LEARNING ABOUT BASIC NEEDS

Finding out how people of other cultures meet their basic needs for food, clothing, and shelter provides some of the most obvious contrasts to our culture.

▶ To broaden your youngster's awareness of how foods differ in other lands, venture together into various ethnic restaurants.

Examples: Most kids have tasted egg rolls, tacos, and spaghetti. Why not try something from Thailand, India, Israel, or Germany?

My son Kevin discovered that he liked Japanese food, especially teriyaki chicken, as well as Chinese food, especially sweet-and-sour pork. Simon, my other son, quickly took to the unusual flavor of Thai tea, a sweet drink he encountered at a Thai restaurant when he was ten.

The genuine ambience in a real foreign restaurant, in contrast to a take-out place, adds something to the experience.

▶ Get a cookbook featuring the foods of one or more other countries. Try out some of the recipes. Shop for ingredients at a grocery store that specializes in foods of that country. Take your time and explore the shop. Ask the grocer questions.

▶ People dress differently in other countries. Library research is recommended for exploring this topic, since pictures are more effective than verbal descriptions.

   Examples: Talk about what it would be like to wear a Scottish kilt, a Polynesian grass skirt, or many layers of cloth, as is the custom in the Arabian desert. Wrap a sheet, sari-style or toga-style, around your daughter or son.

▶ People also live in a variety of structures. How would your life be different if you lived in a house up on stilts as protection from animals? In an igloo? In a mud hut?

   A good book to accompany this discussion is *Charlie Brown's Fourth Super Book of Questions and Answers About All Kinds of People and How They Live.* See Resources, page 160.

▶ Climate affects cultural development much more than most children realize.

   Examples: Talk about different climates and lifestyles within the United States. How might the life of a child in Nome, Alaska, differ from that of a child in Los Angeles, California?

   What if you lived where the night is six months long? Where it rains nearly every day of the year? How would this affect your moods? What if you lived where the days last for months at a time?

EXPLORING CULTURAL ATTITUDES

Attitudes toward childhood, growing up, aging, and death differ widely from society to society. Here are some examples and questions to use as conversation starters with your child.

▶ When a traditional Muslim family is divided by divorce, the children stay with their mother until they are eight years old, at which time they are automatically given over to the custody of their father. Compare this with what happens in the United States.

139

▶ In each of the United States, there's an age at which young people are considered adults, usually eighteen or twenty-one. In many other cultures, certain behavior is required before a child is given the privileges of adulthood. What does your child think it means to be an adult?

▶ In certain societies, the crossing of the line from childhood to adulthood is clearly marked by ceremony and rites of passage.

Examples: In Jewish families, special ceremonies called the bar mitzvah (for boys) and bat mitzvah (for girls) are held when children are around twelve or thirteen years old. Graduation ceremonies are common in many cultures.

In our family and community, an important rite of passage takes place when a sixteen-year-old obtains his driver's license. From that point on, the teenager has a new freedom that dramatically alters his lifestyle.

Think about and discuss any rites of passage your family observes.

▶ Youth is highly valued in American culture, while other countries honor the aged. In many Latin American and Oriental countries, birthdays are big occasions for the elderly, since advancing years bring additional power and prestige. Being called "the old one" is a good thing in these countries.

Ask your child to consider these questions: Is it a good thing or a bad thing to be old in the United States? What is something you could do to honor an elderly person you know?

▶ In American society, death is rarely discussed openly, and children seldom come in contact with it. Elsewhere, death is seen as a natural part of the life process, and all members of the community participate in funerals and mourning.

Has your child ever experienced the death of a pet? How did your family mark the occasion?

If your child has experienced the loss of a relative, was she included in the funeral ceremony? Talk about what she remembers of the event.

▶ Unusual funeral customs are interesting to learn about, and they open the door to conversation.

Examples: Anthropologist Peter A. Metcalf has studied the funeral customs of the Berawan, a small tribe in north central Borneo. The funeral rites are performed immediately after death for a period of two to ten days. Next, the bereaved family stores the corpse on a platform in the grave-yard for at least eight months and up to several years. Then the family brings the corpse back to the longhouse (a communal hall) and entertains guests for six to ten days. During this stage, the family may take the bones of the deceased and clean them. Lastly, the remains are removed to a mausoleum.

This intimate interaction with the dead seems strange to us. Metcalf reported that the Berawan found our customs equally strange, especially the practice of embalming (treating the corpse with preservative fluids).

Consider visiting a funeral home with your child to learn more about the American way of dealing with death.

▶ Different cultures have different norms where privacy is concerned.

Example: The American dream of a room for each child is not universal. In countries with very large families and limited accommodations, many people sleep in the same bedroom and think nothing of it.

As an only child, I always had my own room. My older son, Simon, shared a room with his brother until he turned nine. When he requested his own room, he expressed it this way: "I haven't had any privacy for seven years!"

Do you read your children's mail? Are they allowed to read yours? What is your family's policy about entering closed rooms?

▶ The relatively new discipline of transcultural medicine teaches health-care workers to deal with conflicts of cultural origin. The way people react to pain, as well as their beliefs about medical treatment and death, are deeply ingrained in a culture.

Examples: Women in the West Indies endure the pain of childbirth without complaint. When a West Indian nurse came to the United States, she aggravated her laboring patients by telling them to quit complaining. This was a case in which transcultural medicine was able to help smooth a culture clash.

Certain American Indians won't take red pills for religious reasons. Some people from other countries are put off by the brusqueness of American medicine. They think it's rude when a doctor comes in and immediately begins to examine them. Latinos prefer to start with chit-chat, while Asians seek formal politeness.

Latinos often believe that giving cold liquids to someone with a fever shocks the body, so they may be upset when a doctor recommends orange juice. A doctor aware of transcultural medicine would recommend simply "liquids" instead.

Like different cultures, different families have their own ways of dealing with illness. In your family, do you rest when you are not feeling well, or do you carry on normal activities?

NODDING, NOSE-TAPPING, AND MORE BODY LANGUAGE

Depending on where you are in the world, body language and common gestures mean entirely different things. What's funny or friendly in one culture may be rude, even obscene in another. A gesture meant to comfort may be anxiety-provoking or antagonistic.

Business people and diplomats who travel widely take special courses in understanding these differences. They don't want an important negotiation or meeting interrupted by misunderstandings.

▶ Nodding the head to signify "yes" is not a universal gesture. In parts of Greece, Turkey, and other countries in the Middle East, it means "no." The way we wave "good-bye" is the same way some Middle Eastern cultures indicate "come here."

Suggest that your child make up some entirely new gestures. How about touching the tip of your nose to mean, "I'm curious, please tell me what you're talking about"? Or pulling on your hair to indicate impatience — "When will you ever get off that phone?"

▶ In Britain, people tap the side of their noses to show that something is confidential. Our "OK" sign, where we touch the tip of a forefinger to the tip of the thumb, means "You're worth zero" in France and Belgium and something vulgar in Brazil, parts of Southern Italy, Greece, and Turkey. Placing

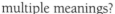

your index finger to the temple, with the other fingers curled, means "That person is smart" in the United States, but "That person is stupid" in Europe. Yet it can also mean the opposite in both places, depending on the verbal context.

Suggest that your child make a collection of gestures he notices people using. Can he think of other gestures with multiple meanings?

▶ Different peoples have different ideas of how close they should be when speaking with one another. In the United States, a man usually stands eighteen to twenty inches from another man while talking, and a few inches farther from a woman. In France and Latin America, people are comfortable standing closer, about thirteen inches from a conversational partner.

Have your child experiment with moving closer than usual when talking with a friend. The friend will most likely back up until the "normal" (for our culture) distance is reestablished.

▶ In Japan, a listener may keep his eyes downcast as a gesture of respect, while Americans look directly at the person to whom they are speaking.

Also in Japan, a listener uses short answers, called *aizuchi,* to show that he's paying attention to a speaker. *Aizuchi* include words like *Ee* (which means "yes"), *Soo-desu-ka* ("Is that so?"), and *Soo-deshoo-ne* ("It must be so.") If the listener doesn't use these words frequently, the speaker feels uneasy.

Can your child think of any equivalents in English? (How about "Hmmm" or "Uh-huh"?)

▶ In an American conversation, when one person is speaking, the other doesn't interrupt. A pause is the cue for the second person to speak. But in France, this cue comes from the tone of the speaker's voice.

Often, children don't know how to enter an ongoing conversation. They interrupt or attract the speaker's attention by fidgeting or by raising their hand, as they're taught to do in school. Practice with your child the "right" way to do this.

TIME TRAVELING

Your child may be surprised to learn that the modern Western concept of linear time has not been shared by all cultures. The Hopi Indians do not even have tenses in their language for past, present, and future.

The subjective experience of time differs for individuals at different phases of the life cycle. The older you are, the faster time seems to go. Eastern mystical religions speak of transcending time to enter eternity.

North Americans are very conscious of the need to be "on time." In other cultures, especially those in southern Europe and Latin America, it's permissible to be late, even for business appointments. When a host in South or Central America wants guests to arrive for an evening meal at 7:30 p.m., he has the option of telling them to come at 7:30 p.m. "American time." Otherwise the guests are likely to arrive closer to 10 p.m.

▶ When California psychologist Robert Levine worked as a visiting professor in Brazil, he noticed that clocks everywhere were set to vastly different times, and that no one seemed to mind. As he reported in the March 1985 issue of *Psychology Today*, he also found that while many students were relaxed about arriving quite late to his classes, many also stayed long after class was over, something his American students seldom did.

A study Levine later carried out showed that Brazilian students defined lateness for lunch as 33 1/2 minutes after the scheduled time, compared to only 19 minutes for students from Fresno. Even the language of the questionnaire he used in his study presented a problem, as the verbs "to wait for," "to hope for," and "to expect" are all translated in Spanish as "esperar."

When you call your child for dinner or to do some chore, how many minutes do you wait before you feel she is "late"? Is her perception the same as yours?

▶ We talk about life in different countries as being "fast-paced" or "slow-paced." In another study Levine carried out to determine a country's "pace of life," he and his researchers measured the accuracy of a country's bank clocks, the speed at which pedestrians walked, and the average time it took a postal clerk to sell a customer a single stamp. Then they ranked different countries around the world.

Japan ranked first, for fastest pace of life. The United States came in second, and England third, with Italy, Taiwan, and Indonesia ranking lowest and slowest.

Unfortunately, it's easy to dismiss people in slower-paced countries as "stupid." Americans who travel in slower-paced countries often become very frustrated.

There are different "paces of life" within the United States. City life is considered faster than country life. Talk about this with your child. What pace is your family used to? What does this have to do with where you live?

▶ Since even children in our society live by the clock, it may be enlightening to spend a weekend day with no reference to time. Cover all the clocks in your home and see what happens.

LEARNING ABOUT THE ARTS

You can learn a lot about a culture by studying its arts. For example, the aesthetics of music vary widely among cultures. The instruments differ, as do the rhythmic and harmonic patterns. Yet there are similarities as well.

While both the Japanese and the Africans play "banjos," both instruments are only vaguely like the American bluegrass banjo. The Chinese and Iranians play "fiddles" which aren't at all like those on which American folk music is played.

In Western music, rhythm is usually a regular pulse, divided into regular groups. In the music of sub-Saharan Africa, the rhythms are extremely complex.

We may think the music of certain nations is "out of tune" when their tuning system and musical scales are merely different from ours. In the Orient, the stress is on pitch and tiny, intricate intervals. Most Indian classical music has a solo melody line, a rhythmic accompaniment, and a drone. Much African music is primarily percussive, played on drums, rattles, bells, and gongs.

What are some similarities? Composer and conductor Leonard Bernstein has spent a lifetime studying music from around the world. He believes there might be a worldwide "musical grammar" — a language all cultures speak. He gives a fascinating example: Children all over the world, on every continent and in every culture, tease each other with the exact same two or three notes, the ones we use to sing or yell "Allee, Allee, in free!"

To find out more about Bernstein's theory, read his book, *The Unanswered Question: Six Talks at Harvard* (Harvard University Press, 1976).

▶ See if your library has selections of music from the Middle East, the Far East, or Africa to share with your child. If not, well-stocked music stores always carry a variety of foreign albums, cassettes, and compact discs.

▶ Music appreciation is mostly learned. We tend to like songs that resemble other songs we like. Does the music your child prefers have the same rhythm and beat as the music you like?

▶ Encourage your child to create homemade instruments.

Examples: Make an African-style xylophone from pieces of wood set across a cardboard shoe box; play it with a pencil. Pot and pan lids can easily double as gongs like those used in Southeast Asia. Panpipes used by Peruvian Indians can be approximated by joining together a series of different-sized tubes. Stretch a string across a board, raised slightly at the ends by bridges; this resembles the Appalachian dulcimer or the ancient Egyptian monochord. Drums can easily be made from coffee tins and other cylindrical containers. Fashion a flute or a whistle by blowing across the top of a pop bottle.

▶ When your child is a competent reader, take her to see a foreign film. Once she's accustomed to the subtitles, she'll begin to observe differences between films made abroad and those we're used to seeing.

Discuss movies as culture clues: How are personal relationships shown? How does the movie deal with violence? What does the movie show you about the country and period in which it was made?

Notice the slower pacing of certain foreign filmmakers such as Herzog and Kurosawa. To a youthful audience used

to fast foods, "Sesame Street," and MTV, Herzog's filming of a ship floating down the Amazon in *Fitzcarraldo* seems abnormally, even agonizingly slow.

) Reading literature from other lands opens more doors. Find some Arabic or Japanese fables, for example. The rich folklore of other countries may come as a surprise to a child raised solely on the Brothers Grimm and the simplified, "cleaned-up" versions of fairy tales found in many children's books.

) Explore other arts with your child. Learn about mask-making as practiced by Native Americans, South Americans, Africans, and others. Find out about the martial arts, which hold a special position in some cultures. (Young children especially will wonder how something that looks like fighting can be called an "art.") Your child might like to take a class in one of the martial arts.

) In the Islamic religion, it's forbidden to use images of living creatures in art. That's why much of Moslem graphic art consists of non-realistic-looking floral themes, geometric figures, and Arabic script.

See if your child can draw a picture using geometric figures and the shapes of letters in artistic ways.

) If possible, take your child to see an Oriental dance troupe. Oriental dancers use facial expressions and hand gestures to communicate the message of the dance.

Suggest that your child make up and perform a dance in which facial expressions and hand gestures tell a story, with a minimum of foot movement.

WHEN HELLO MEANS GOOD-BYE: LEARNING ABOUT LANGUAGE

) *Aloha* means both hello and good-bye in Hawaiian. *Shalom*, which actually means peace, is used also as hello and good-bye in Hebrew.

Obtain a language book that includes words from a variety of languages. With your children, learn how to say hello or some other common word in a number of languages. Observe the similarities and differences.

▶ Introduce your youngster to the concept of an international language. The more than 40,000 members of the Universal Esperanto Association speak Esperanto, which uses mostly Latin roots and has a consistent, logical grammar.

Examples: Nouns always end in the letter "o," adjectives with "a." Plurals of nouns are formed by adding "j," pronounced like the "y" in toy. Root words are combined into words like "horsehouse," which quite sensibly means the place where a horse lives (instead of a stable). Hello is "salu-ton." "The pen is blue" becomes "La pumo estas blua."

▶ Some languages have a variety of words for what English speakers think of as a single entity, such as the Eskimos' almost 170 versions of "ice." Since ice is so important in their lives, Eskimos differentiate among the various kinds, from slush ice to black ice. In *They Have A Word For It: A Lighthearted Lexicon of Untranslatable Words and Phrases*, Howard Rheingold explains this phenomenon and gives interesting examples of Eskimo ice-words. See Resources, page 165.

Have your child choose something important to her — stickers, ice cream, or telephones, for example — and make up a variety of words for different kinds.

▶ Every society has evolved words to soothe its infants, with most lullabies depending on monotonous sounds and rhythms for their calming effect. *Lull* comes from Roman times, when the word *lalla* was used to quiet babies.

Here are some examples of the lull-words used in lullabies around the world: *Ai lu lu* (Poland), *Arroro ro ro* (Spanish-speaking countries), *A-ya ya* (Trinidad), *Baloo, baloo* (Scotland), *Bayu bayu* (Russia), *Bom pe, bom pe* (Cambodia), *Ma ma ma* (Yuma Indian, United States), *Nen nen* (France, Japan), *Shoheen-shal-eo* (Ireland), *Su su su su* (Estonia, Poland, Ukraine, Sweden), *Yo yo yo yo* (the Bantu tribe of Africa).

Make up a new lullabye with your child, using some of the lull-words.

▶ Discuss examples of how language affects social values, and vice versa. In Chinese, for example, there is no word for

privacy. Also, *ying*, a common Chinese word, is translated as either "ought" or "must." In English, these two concepts are quite different.

▶ In the late 1980s, Dr. Vitaly Shevoroshkin, a Soviet linguist at the University of Michigan, studied 140 European and Asian languages in order to determine if there ever existed a common ancestral language from which all others have descended. After locating the fifteen oldest, most stable words in all the languages, he theorized that these words were in the vocabulary of a common language spoken 12,000 years ago.

See if your child can guess which fifteen words he discovered.

(*Answer:* The 15 words stand for the following concepts: I/me, two/pair, thou/thee/you, who/what, tongue, name, eye, heart, tooth, no/not, fingernail/toenail, louse, tear [as in crying], water, and dead.)

GODS AND GARDENS: COMPARATIVE MYTHOLOGY

Comparative mythology in its simplest form — learning how diverse cultures have developed similar myths to explain how the world works — is worth introducing to school-age children. Though this is a complex subject, it's important to understand that the myths we are raised with aren't the only ones, and that all cultures have their own myths, equally meaningful to them.

▶ The works of Joseph Campbell are recommended reading for the parent who would converse knowledgeably on the topic. Or watch the six-videotape set of the PBS series, "Joseph Campbell and The Power of Myth with Bill Moyers," for a fascinating and comprehensible tour of comparative mythology. See Resources, page 163.

▶ Timeless symbols appear in myth, and also in our dreams. These show up frequently in works of art from around the world.

Examples: A Garden of Eden appears in the mythologies of many cultures, as do flood myths. The snake of Judeo-

Christian legend is a life bringer in the myths of other cultures; a cobra protects the Buddha while he meditates.

Look for these common symbols the next time you visit an art museum with your child: An egg stands for creation or rebirth; a sun rising also means rebirth; a sunset may mean death; a lighted candle represents the brevity of life; milk and water represent life; children symbolize innocence; sheep stand for gentleness; clowns symbolize the imagination, or the childish side of the personality.

▶ While Christians and Jews learn that "in the beginning" the world was dark until God said "let there be light," children in the Banks Islands of Melanesia learn another description for the beginning of the world: "In the beginning, there was light. It never dimmed, this light over everything." This and other creation tales may be found in the book, *In the Beginning: Creation Stories From Around the World*; see Resources, page 163.

▶ Before or after doing some research on creation myths, suggest that you and your child brainstorm all the ways he thinks the world might have started. Encourage him to develop the most imaginative creation myth he can.

■ ■ ■ ■ ■ ■ ■ ■ ■ ■ ■ ■ ■ ■ ■ ■ ■ ■ ■ ■

FAMILY FOLKLORE

Don't forget that your own family has a history and a folklore. By discussing what you know of these, you'll be teaching your child that your family is like others around the world.

Suggest that your child interview you and her grandparents, using a tape recorder or video camera. She can make up her own questions or use these to start with:

1. "What country did our family come from?"

2. "Do we celebrate special occasions like births, weddings, funerals, and holidays the same way people do in that country?"

3. "How did you celebrate holidays when you were young? What special games or food can you remember?"

4. "Do you know any dances or songs from 'the old country'?"

5. "Do you have any old costumes, toys, crafts, or recipes?"

Recording Your Family History: A Guide to Preserving Oral History Using Audio and Video Tape by William Fletcher (Ten Speed Press, 1989) is an incredibly detailed handbook for the serious interviewer of any age.

TWELVE MORE WAYS TO APPRECIATE CULTURAL DIVERSITY

1. Contact the international student adviser at your local university. He or she may be able to introduce you to a foreign student so your child can gain first-hand knowledge of a different culture.

   Invite the student to dinner or on an outing with your family. Perhaps he or she could show your child how to prepare a simple recipe from home.

2. Hang up a map of the world where everyone in your family can see it. Buy a globe, if you don't already have one. Now you're ready for any number of activities.

   Examples: Make a point of locating countries in the news, and countries you read about as you discuss cultural diversity. Compare the globe to a standard flat map and notice how the shapes of the countries are different on each. (A globe shows countries in a more accurate relationship geographically than a map.)

   Turn the map or globe upside down and see how that affects your perceptions of the world. Does it make a difference when South America is above North America, or Africa is above Europe? An Australian company publishes a map called "McArthur's Universal Corrective Map of the World," in which Australia is in the center.

3. Close your eyes, spin the globe, and see which country your pointing finger stops on. Research that country and choose one of its customs to observe for an hour or a day.

4. Finding yourself in an alien environment can be very disconcerting. Almost everyone who emigrates from one country to another has this experience.

   Use role play to help your child understand what it means to switch cultures. One or both of you can pretend you are newly arrived in this country. Walk around the house and exclaim at whatever is strange: the appliances, the food, the clothing.

5. Your family may be willing to try what students in a Colorado elementary school did: To increase awareness of world hunger, students were given color-coded tickets at lunchtime. Different colors represented different areas of the world, and the students received meals representative of those areas. The Asian lunch was a bowl of rice and a glass of water; the African lunch was a bowl of green beans and water; the South American meal was beans and rice with water.

6. Discuss with your child how American culture of today is different than it was one, two, or five generations ago. This home-based historical perspective adds insight to the study of worldwide cultural differences.

7. Get copies of foreign periodicals from other English-speaking countries, such as Canada, Australia, or England. The subtle differences in the way the language is used will be instructive.

   A company called Multinewspapers offers single copies and subscriptions for English-language newspapers published around the world, from Iceland to Fiji, Athens to Australia. Write: Multinewspapers, Box DE, Dana Point, California 92629.

8. Ask to be placed on the mailing lists of local colleges and universities. When they hold ethnic events or exhibits, you'll know about them and can attend with your child.

9. Visit art, anthropology, and specialized ethnic museums with your family.

10. Encourage your child to go Trick-or-Treating for UNICEF. For information about obtaining collection cartons, educational brochures, and other materials, write to: U.S.

Committee for UNICEF, 333 East 38th St., New York, New York 10016.

This would make a rewarding activity for a small group of your child's friends. By collecting for UNICEF on Halloween, youngsters become aware of the plight of many children in developing countries. In 1988, for example, UNICEF immunized over 1.5 million children and helped save a million young lives by the use of low-cost oral rehydration therapy.

Another fact: A baby born in 1981 in Nepal could expect to live to be 45 years old, while a baby born in 1981 in Canada could expect to live to be 75 years old.

11. Visit a travel agency and collect brochures on foreign countries. Plan an imaginary trip to another country. Take into consideration what kind of clothing you'd need for that country's climate.

12. Pick a country or two and follow it closely in the newspaper and in news magazines.

■ ■ ■ ■ ■ ■ ■ ■ ■ ■ ■ ■ ■ ■ ■ ■ ■ ■ ■ ■

PEN PALS: THE WRITE STUFF

Exchanging letters with someone in a foreign land offers many benefits to any child. It's a great way to learn about different customs, broaden one's perspective, improve letter-writing skills, have fun exchanging postcards, photos, and souvenirs, and maybe even make a lifelong friend.

You can help your child to get a pen pal in another country. Here are four places to start:

▸ Student Letter Exchange. For ages 10–21. For an application, send a SASE to: 215 5th Ave., SE, Waseca, Minnesota 56093.

▸ Information Center on Children's Cultures, The U.S. Committee for UNICEF, 331 E. 38th St., New York, New York 10016. For a SASE, this agency will provide you with a list of pen pal agencies around the world. Also request their flyer, "Helpful tips for good letter writing to children in other countries," which offers suggestions on abbreviations (don't use them, except for "Mr." and "Mrs."), slang and colloquial expressions (avoid them), bragging (don't), and more. It also includes numerous ideas on what to write about (extra-curricular activities, where you spend your vacations, what you typically eat, what your parents do, what holidays you celebrate, and so on).

▶ "Via Air Mail: Your Guide to Overseas Penpals" is an eight-page pamphlet which lists American and overseas sources for obtaining pen pals and gives hints on writing to foreign pen pals. For more information, write: BeauBee Enterprises, P.O. Box 238, Olympia Fields, Illinois 60461.

▶ Kids Meeting Kids Can Make a Difference is an organization devoted to matching up American and Soviet pen pals ages 7–18. Write: Kids Meeting Kids, Box 8H, 380 Riverside Dr., New York, New York 10025. Or call (212) 662-2327.

■ ■ ■ ■ ■ ■ ■ ■ ■ ■ ■ ■ ■ ■ ■ ■ ■ ■ ■ ■

HOLIDAYS AROUND THE WORLD

Every culture has its own unique holidays and celebrations. Even those that are widely celebrated are observed differently by different peoples.

The U.S. Committee for UNICEF offers a wall calendar showing national, religious, and family holidays celebrated by United Nations member nations. For example: On a Saturday in May, the children in the Netherlands celebrate Luilak, which means "lazybones." Early in the morning, children all over the country gather in groups and walk through towns, making as much noise as possible to wake up the "lazybones" and trick the "winter demon" into going away. See Resources, page 166.

Most of us know the story of Christmas; some of us also know and celebrate Chanukah, the Jewish Festival of Lights. But how many of us are aware of the Hindu Festival of Lights? Called Divali (also spelled Dipawali), it's observed in the fall and culminates a holiday that lasts nearly two weeks. Although the practices of Hinduism vary by region, most Hindus consider Lakshmi, the goddess of prosperity, to be the main patroness of

the festival. Merchants begin their New Year from this point. People light lamps inside and outside their homes. Believers build a temporary altar inside their homes, then place coins and other symbols of wealth on it. Sweets are exchanged.

December 26 marks the start of Kwanzaa, a seven-day holiday for black families to celebrate their African-American heritage. Kwanzaa means "first" in Swahili. The holiday, introduced in the United States in 1966, gets its rituals from African harvest festivals. On each of the seven days, a family member explains one of the principles on which the celebration is based (unity, self-determination, collective work and responsibility, cooperative economics, purpose, creativity, and faith) and how he or she practices it. Gifts relating to black culture are given to children, and on December 31 an African feast is held. Does your community have any festivities to mark Kwanzaa?

The Chinese New Year is a traditional spring festival that is celebrated by the Chinese in the United States for a week or two or more. Find out what "year" it was when your child was born; 1990 ushered in "Year of the Horse."

Tet is the seven-day celebration of the Vietnamese New Year and of spring. The word is an abbreviation of Tet Nguyen-Dan, which means "first day."

Cinco de Mayo (the "Fifth of May") celebrates the day in May of 1862 when Mexicans defeated invading French forces.

Here are more ethnic celebrations you can commemorate: Pan American Day (April 14), Asian-Pacific American Heritage Week (the first week in May), American Indian Day (usually the fourth Friday in September), Japanese Girls' Doll Festival (March 3), Oktoberfest (starts September 21), Greek Independence Day (March 25).

GLOBAL GAME-PLAYING

Learning about the variety of sports and games played around the world can be a fascinating topic to research with your child.

What we know as soccer is called football in many other countries. Kickball is played as a spiritual ceremony among the Hopi Indians of the southwestern United States. There's another game called Indian kickball (played by the Tarahumara Indians of northern Mexico) in which an oak root ball or stone ball is kicked by teams of three to six players along a course of twenty to forty miles.

A Chinese game called "Helping Harvest the Land" is symbolic of the communal living in the People's Republic of China. Two teams of four members each line up at the same side of the play area, which should ideally be dirt, with the equipment — a toy hoe, watering can, tricycle, and plastic flowers — at the opposite side. The first team member runs across the play area, picks up a hoe and hoes the ground five times, then returns to his or her team. The second team member plants the flowers and runs back. The third waters the flowers, and the fourth picks the flowers, places them in the tricycle's basket, then rides the trike back. The first team to complete the cycle wins.

"London Bridge" has variations in other countries. In Italy it's called "Open the Gates." In Latin America it's played with a fruit theme: Each player is given the name of a fruit, which must be kept secret. The arch (made by players' hands) is dropped on the person suspected of being the fruit being sung

about ("Here's a woman selling apples, selling apples, selling apples..."). If the guess is wrong, the player is released.

▶ Some of the games we play today have long histories and are played on homemade equipment in other cultures. Tic-tac-toe and tug-of-war are seen everywhere. Dominoes was invented by the Chinese at least three centuries ago. Modern European dominoes contains twenty-eight pieces, including blanks. Chinese dominoes has thirty-two pieces and no blanks. Eskimos play with walrus-ivory dominoes which are marked with higher values but played like European dominoes.

Consider modifying a set of dominoes to imitate the way these other cultures play the game.

▶ "Cat's Cradle" is played in almost every country of the world, with people in widely separated regions making some of the same string figures. The Japanese and the Chugach Eskimos call it a girls' game, but Navaho Indian men are expert at weaving string figures.

If neither you nor your child knows how to play Cat's Cradle, find someone who can teach you.

▶ "Muk," an Eskimo game from the Canadian Arctic, means "silence." Players sit in a circle. One player enters the middle of the circle and points to another player. That person must say "Muk" and then remain silent and straight-faced while the person in the middle uses gestures and expressions in an effort to make him or her laugh. If the pointer succeeds, the laugher replaces him or her in the middle.

Consider playing this game at your child's next birthday party.

▶ Playing "Know Your Potato" is a good way for children to learn to appreciate individual difference. Each person selects a potato and looks at it closely. Then everyone dumps their potatoes in a pile, mixes them up, and each of you tries to find "your" potato. The point is, although all potatoes may look alike, you'll discover differences that make each one unique.

SHORTWAVE: LONG ON EDUCATIONAL VALUE

Introduce your child to shortwave radio. Listening to international broadcasts is another way to get in touch with the larger world outside. These broadcasts originate in a variety of world capitals, and many are in English.

When your child notes on a map the countries whose shortwave signals she has picked up, her knowledge of geography improves. When she tunes in regularly, she can't help learning about current events, history, and the music of other nations, as well as hearing foreign languages.

There's something immediate and real about hearing someone speaking from a faraway place and knowing that it's happening at this moment. Children often respond by wanting to know more about these other countries.

A simple shortwave without digital tuning costs as little as $60, and ones with digital tuning start at about $125. (Check your local *Yellow Pages* under "Radio Communications Equipment" or "Amateur Radio Dealers.") While learning to tune the shortwave isn't difficult, there are other more challenging aspects as you go along. Here are two books that offer help. Both are available from Tiare Publications, P.O. Box 493, Lake Geneva, Wisconsin 53147; telephone (414) 248-4845.

▸ *So You Bought a Shortwave Radio! A Get Acquainted Guide to the Wide World of Shortwave* by Gerry L. Dexter. Covers the basics for beginners, including where to find listings of English-language foreign broadcasts.

▸ *Shortwave Goes to School — A Teacher's Guide to Using Shortwave Radio in the Classroom* by Myles Mustoe. Most of these activities for ages ten and up are adaptable for home use. They include comparing the way a major news story is handled by broadcasters in different countries, discovering jargon, and mailing reception reports to stations and seeing what comes back in the mail (stickers, magazines, maps, and so on). This book also lists several equipment dealers.

RESOURCES

Art from Many Hands by Jo Miles Schuman (Davis Publications, 1981). Art activities from many cultures for elementary to high school. Step-by-step instructions and plentiful illustrations.

Best-Loved Folk-Tales of the World selected by Joanna Cole (Doubleday, 1982). This anthology of more than 200 folk and fairy tales from around the world provides ample proof of the universality of certain themes across cultural and historical lines. Includes indexes by category and title.

The Boy From Over There by Tamar Bergman, translated from the Hebrew by Hillel Halkin (Houghton Mifflin, 1988). For ages 10–14. This novel explores the feelings of a Holocaust survivor who is a newcomer to an Israeli kibbutz in the days before the first Arab-Israeli war.

Chang's Paper Pony by Eleanor Coerr (Harper & Row, 1988). For ages 4–8. This "I Can Read Book" tells the story of immigrants from China to California in Gold Rush days, illustrating the feeling of loneliness that is so common to strangers in a new land.

Charlie Brown's Fourth Super Book of Questions and Answers About All Kinds of People and How They Live (Random House, 1979). Full of facts about people around the world, yesterday and today — holidays, clothing, how the places they live have affected their ways of life. Illustrated with the "Charlie Brown" comic strip characters, it's suitable for very young children as well as those who can read it on their own.

"Coretta Scott King Award and Honor Books" is a brochure from the American Library Association. Each year, the ALA publishes a booklist recognizing African-American authors and illustrators whose works carry on the legacy of Dr. Martin Luther King, Jr., by emphasizing understanding and appreciation of the culture and the contributions of all its people. The brochure lists the winners from 1970 to the present. Write: Library Outreach Services, Re: Coretta Scott King Award and Honor Books, ALA, 50 E. Huron St., Chicago, Illinois 60611. Be sure to include a SASE.

Courage Children's Illustrated World Atlas (Running Press, 1989). Illustrated with over 600 full-color pictures and maps, this atlas helps young people understand their place in the larger world, with sections that build up from the most familiar environment (the child's room and house) to travel and communications around the world. The major part of the book deals with individual countries, featuring photos and data about towns, products, population, currency, flags, language, and more.

"Culturgrams" are four-page brochures, each describing the customs, manners, and lifestyles of one of 96 countries. For example, the Culturgram on the Republic of Singapore states that great respect is paid to the elderly, and that it's polite on buses to give one's seat to an elderly person; that shoes are removed before entering most religious buildings; and that one should never beckon using only one finger. For more information, write: Brigham Young University David M. Kennedy Center for International Studies, Publication Services, 280 HRCB, Provo, Utah 84602. Or call (801) 378-6528.

EarthBeat!, Box 1460, Redway, California 95560; toll-free telephone 1-800-346-4445. The goal of this catalog is "to explore and celebrate diversity," with a special focus on music. Recordings include American folk singers, African songs of liberation, Persian soul, Polynesian dance, Latin American bards, and more. The catalog also features crafts and musical instruments. Request a free copy.

"Ethnic Cultures of America Calendar," published annually for several years, notes more than 200 holidays celebrated by ethnic groups in the United States (Last Day of Ramadan, Buddha Day, Baltic Freedom Day, Green Corn Dance Day). "World Calendar" notes religious holidays (each explained in an index), birthdays of significant world leaders, and civil holidays of about 100 countries. It also includes international tips of various kinds in the back. Each calendar measures 11" x 14". Write: Educational Extension Systems, P.O. Box 259, Clarks Summit, Pennsylvania 18411. Or call toll-free 1-800-447-8561.

Faces: The Magazine about People. This periodical covers a variety of topics in cultural anthropology and archaeology for ages 8–14. Issues are built around a theme and include stories, articles, crafts, recipes, and games. Ten issues per year. Write: Cobblestone Publishing Co., 30 Grove St., Peterborough, New Hampshire 03458. Or call (603) 924-7209. To order, call toll-free 1-800-341-1522.

Families: A Celebration of Diversity, Commitment, and Love by Aylette Jennes (Houghton Mifflin, 1990). Seventeen young people describe their families in their own words, illustrated by the author's photographs. Some families contain adopted children, some are stepfamilies, others are ethnically or religiously mixed, one contains a mother who is deaf. Inspiring for all ages.

Families the World Over series (Lerner, 1985-1990). For ages 7–10. Each 32-page book in this series focuses on a country: *An Aboriginal Family, An Arab Family, A Family in France, A Family in Nigeria,* and so on. Also from the same publisher is the In America series of 32 titles

including *The Lebanese in America*, *The Puerto Ricans in America*, etc. For ages 10 and up, each is 64–124 pages. Request a catalog from: Lerner Publications Co., 241 First Avenue North, Minneapolis, Minnesota 55401. Or call toll-free 1-800-328-4929. In Minnesota, call collect (612) 332-3344.

Friends Around the World. This game by Joan Walsh Anglund is for 2–4 players ages 5 and up. Children race their 16 international friends (each complete with biographical information) toward world peace. This is a cooperative game: everyone wins or loses together. "Where in the World?" is a world awareness game for 2–6 players ages 8 to adult. It contains 174 country cards and may be played in a variety of ways. Both games are available from Aristoplay, Ltd. Call toll-free 1-800-634-7738; in Michigan, call (313) 995-4353. Request a catalog.

Games of the World: How to Make Them, How to Play Them, How They Came to Be, edited by Frederic V. Grunfeld (Holt, Rinehart and Winston, 1975). A colorful compendium of games of the world, with instructions for making them. Includes history and folklore of many nations.

Give Peace a Chance: A Game of International Relations and Conflict Resolution is for 2-4 players ages 9 to adult. Players choose to be countries which gain or lose peace tokens depending on game board directions. Children think about peace, become aware of global interdependence, and learn to negotiate with other players (suggestions on how to negotiate are included). Write: Peace Works, Inc., 3812 N. First, Fresno, California 93726. Or call (209) 435-8092. Request a flyer listing related products.

Growing Up Amish by Richard Ammon (Atheneum, 1989). For ages 7–12. This true story of Anna, an Amish girl, includes photographs, recipes, songs, poems, and games to help young readers better understand these people.

The Hero with a Thousand Faces by Joseph Campbell (Princeton University Press, 1949). This superb introduction to comparative mythology is a must for parents who want to explore the topic in depth with their older children.

Human Relations Materials for the School from the Anti-Defamation League of B'nai B'rith. This catalog contains some materials equally suitable for use by parents and children at home, such as "Your Neighbor Worships," a 31-page guided tour of the synagogue. Write: Anti-Defamation League of B'nai B'rith, 823 United Nations Plaza, New York, New York 10017.

The Igloo by Charlotte and David Yue (Houghton Mifflin, 1988). Interesting facts and details about Eskimo homes and lives, showing how they have adapted to their incredibly cold environment. Many illustrations.

Information Center on Children's Cultures, The U.S. Committee for UNICEF, 331 E. 38th St., New York, New York 10016. This center contains a collection of educational and cultural materials in English about children of other lands. It also houses primary source materials, usually in the language of their respective countries, that have been created for, about, and by children from many lands. The center answers questions from individuals about how to get a pen pal, what is the significance of a children's holiday celebrated in a particular country, where to get children's books in another language, and so on. Send a SASE for a flyer naming "Book Lists, Information Sheets and Teaching Units." These cover such topics as holidays and festivals, Christmas around the world, shelter around the world, children's books, and songs and dances of the world.

In the Beginning: Creation Stories From Around the World told by Virginia Hamilton (Harcourt Brace Jovanovich, 1988). For ages 8 and up. This illustrated volume contains 25 stories from many cultures, showing the different ways each of them has explained the genesis of the world or of humankind. Includes 42 full-color paintings and author comments.

In Two Worlds: A Yup'ik Eskimo Family by Aylette Jenness and Alice Rivers (Houghton Mifflin Co., 1989). For ages 10–14 . This is the true story of how Alice and Billy Rivers and their children live in the small Alaskan community of Scammon Bay, where they combine modern technology with traditional ways. Illustrated with black and white photos; contains an appendix of resources for further investigation.

"Joseph Campbell and The Power of Myth with Bill Moyers." The six-videotape set of the PBS series takes you on a fascinating and comprehensible tour of comparative mythology. Your video store may carry these tapes. If not, write: Mystic Fire Video, P.O. Box 9323, S. Burlington, Vermont 05403. Or call toll-free 1-800-727-8433.

The Land I Lost: Adventures of a Boy in Vietnam by Huynh Quang Nhuong, with pictures by Vo-Dinh Mai (Harper & Row, 1982). For ages 9–12. This book of true stories was written by a graduate of Saigon University who was paralyzed by a gunshot wound after being drafted into the South Vietnamese army. The chapters tell of his boyhood memories of his tiny hamlet, including vignettes about various relatives, crocodiles, pythons, and a pet water buffalo.

Little Daniel and the Jewish Delicacies by Smadar Shir Sidi (Adama Books, 1988). For ages 3–10. A little boy eats his way through a year's worth of Jewish holidays in hopes of growing taller. In the process, he learns the meanings of the various foods and religious customs.

My Friends' Beliefs: A Young Reader's Guide to World Religions by Hiley H. Ward (Walker and Company, 1988). For ages 10–14. Highlights the beliefs of young worshipers around the United States, from George Demos, a 10-year-old Greek Orthodox boy in New York, to James Martin, a 15-year-old Buddhist monk in Maryland. Much detail, entertainingly presented. Also includes an appendix of addresses to write to for more information about the various well- and lesser-known religions, maps, and an index.

National Geographic World is a full-color monthly magazine for ages 8–12. Features well-written articles on nature, animals, science, sports, and oddities of interest to children, plus things to make and do. Write: National Geographic World, Box 2330, Washington, D.C. 20013.

Nicole Visits an Amish Farm, a photo story by Erika Stone, text by Merle Good (Walker and Company, 1985). For ages 5–10. City girl Nicole spends two weeks on an Amish farm in Pennsylvania, learning how a rural family with no TV spends its time in games and chores.

People by Peter Spier (Doubleday, 1980). This richly illustrated, over-sized picture book is suitable for ages 3 or 4 and up. Spier demonstrates the diversity among the earth's four billion people, comparing eye shape, children's games, forms of shelter, occupations, religious beliefs, and more.

"Shalom Sesame" is a series of five 30-minute videos about Israel for ages 2–12. Narrated by Itzhak Perlman and Bonnie Franklin, it features familiar and new "Sesame Street" Muppet characters (who sometimes speak Hebrew). These are beautifully made programs, featuring scenery from around Israel and a variety of ethnic groups including religious and non-religious Jews, Israeli Arabs, and Druse. The set comes with a 40-page "Family Viewing Guide." Write: The American Friends of Rechov Sumsum, 1 Lincoln Plaza, 4th Floor, New York, New York 10023. Or call (212) 595-9132.

"Sharing Through Music: A Multicultural Experience" is a booklet describing traditional stringed instruments from various nations. Available free from Marvi Ricker, University of Toronto, 21 King's College Circle, 2nd floor, Toronto, Ontario M5S 1A1, Canada.

Shelters: From Tepee to Igloo by Harvey Weiss (Thomas Y. Crowell, 1988). For ages 10–13. Presents a historical and modern look at shelters around the world, including how they are constructed and why each is the perfect adaptation to a particular environment and set of cultural needs.

Skipping Stones: A Multi-ethnic Children's Forum is an excellent publication that is trying to change the world by teaching children to appreciate diversity. Children from diverse backgrounds share experiences through their stories, poems, and artwork; games and activities are included to help them learn to compare and contrast various cultures. Published quarterly. Write: Skipping Stones, 80574 Hazelton Rd., Cottage Grove, Oregon 97424. Or call (503) 942-9434.

Small World Celebrations by Jean Warren and Elizabeth McKinnon (Warren Publishing House, 1988). For parents of children ages 3–5. How to celebrate 16 international holidays through art activities, learning games, songs, and snacks. Learn about Lei Day, Saint Patrick's Day, Chinese New Year, Inter-Tribal Indian Ceremonial, and more.

Social Studies School Service publishes Global Education and Geography catalogs that contain multi-cultural materials suitable for home use by parents and children. (An example: *Do's and Taboos Around the World* by Roger E. Axtell.) Write: 10200 Jefferson Blvd., P.O. Box 802, Culver City, California 90232-0802. Or call toll-free 1-800-421-4246.

Somehow Tenderness Survives: Stories of Southern Africa selected by Hazel Rochman (Harper & Row, 1988). This is a collection of ten short stories by well-known writers (Doris Lessing, Nadine Gordimer, and others) who tell what it's like to grow up under apartheid. The publisher's age recommendation is 12 and up, but this book is also appropriate for some 9- or 10-year-olds. Grim, enlightening, and unfortunately still necessary.

Song of Sedna by Robert D. San Souci, pictures by Daniel San Souci (Doubleday, 1989). For ages 5–10. One version of the Eskimo myth in which a maiden named Sedna is transformed into the goddess of the sea, who aids fishermen and hunters.

They Have A Word For It: A Lighthearted Lexicon of Untranslatable Words and Phrases by Howard Rheingold (Jeremy P. Tarcher, 1988). This book is a cross-cultural education, full of useful words for which there are no equivalents in English.

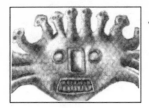

Tortillitas Para Mama and Other Nursery Rhymes in Spanish and English, selected and translated by Margot C. Griego, Betsy L. Bucks, Sharon S. Gilbert, and Laurel H. Kimball, illustrated by Barbara Cooney (Henry Holt & Co., 1981). This is a collection of Latin American nursery rhymes for young children that have been passed from generation to generation. Many are accompanied by instructions for finger play.

The Travelers' Guide to Asian Customs and Manners by Kevin Chambers (Meadowbrook, 1988). A handy manual detailing do's and don'ts for 16 Asian countries. For example, you'll learn that it's impolite for a man to wink at a woman in Australia, and it's rude to say "thank you" when complimented in South Korea — you should deny the compliment.

U.S. Committee for UNICEF, 475 Oberlin Ave. South, CN 2110, Lakewood, New Jersey 08701; toll-free telephone 1-800-553-1200. Request their Cards, Gifts, and Stationery catalog, which includes games, books, puzzles, and a wall calendar noting holidays around the world.

"Video Letter from Japan" is a series of six video packages suitable for ages 9 and up. Individual titles cover a day in the life of a Tokyo sixth-grader, a look at two families in northern Japan, school life in Japan, and other subjects. Each 25-minute video comes with a teacher's manual and poster. There are also three videos in the "Discover Korea" series. Write: The Asia Society, 725 Park Ave., New York, New York 10021-5088. Or call (212) 288-6400.

CHAPTER 11
The Junior Psychologist

The science of psychology has many branches, all of which are involved with some aspect of studying behavior. From sleep researchers who study dreams, to experimental psychologists who work in the field and lab, to social psychologists who study how people act in groups, all psychologists work at understanding people's complexities.

While courses in psychology are rarely taught before college level, much about this fascinating field lends itself perfectly to parent/child discussion and exploration. After all, what could be more interesting to people than themselves?

DREAMWORK

For several months around the time of his parents' divorce, Simon spent his nights flying. During the day, the fifth-grader was caught up in conflicts between his mother and father, but once asleep, he simply waved his arms and took off.

Simon enjoyed the incredible feeling of freedom and of being in complete control. In some dreams, however, arm-flapping didn't work, and Simon had to stay on the ground and face whatever came along.

Kevin had loved the idleness of summer. A few days before he was to begin junior high school, he dreamed he came to school unprepared. He had to take tests he knew nothing about. He didn't know anyone, and he couldn't find his locker.

Kevin woke up relieved that it had only been a dream, and immediately asked his mother to take him shopping for some new notebooks and school clothes.

Talking about dreams is a good way to begin introducing your child to the workings of the human mind. Dreams are a universal human experience that begins in infancy, and they have a way of bringing out feelings that might not otherwise find expression. By helping your child tune into his dreams and discuss them with you, you're also giving him a safe means for communicating his feelings.

Start by sharing these facts, if your child is interested: The younger the child, the more time he or she spends dreaming. While newborns dream 45–65 percent of their sleep time, or 9 hours a day, a child two to five years old dreams about 2 hours. A child five to thirteen years old spends 15–20 percent of sleep time dreaming, and the average adult who sleeps 8 hours spends 1 of them dreaming.

It seems that at least two-thirds of the dreams children recall are negative ones, so don't panic if all your youngster can tell you about are bad dreams. The incidence of nightmares tends to peak between ages five and seven, when the child is going to school for the first time and is subject to many demands. Bad dreams also appear to be more memorable. The happy, adventurous dreams, as well as the mundane ones, are more easily lost upon awakening.

According to most experts, it's important not to try to interpret children's dreams for them. When they're ready, they'll make the connection themselves. In fact, if you rush in with your own meanings, your child may feel threatened. The right time to ask a few helpful questions is when she shows some interest in why she had a particular dream and you have an idea to contribute.

Dreams make their own sense of what is going on in a child's life. Just as with adults, a child's dream of food may relate to attitudes about one's parents, or it may just mean the dreamer is hungry. The dreaming mind changes things around, which is one reason why so many creative ideas come out of the dreaming state. Each of us develops our own dream symbols, the significance of which we may not be able to grasp easily. Beware of simplistic, one-symbol-fits-all interpretations.

■ ■ ■ ■ ■ ■ ■ ■ ■ ■ ■ ■ ■ ■ ■ ■ ■ ■ ■ ■

PLANTS AND PAJAMAS: A DREAM ANALYZED

The McDermotts were getting ready to move to a larger home in a nearby neighborhood. Four-year-old Rory asked, "Are we going to be taking our plants?" Her father reassured her that they would.

Two days later Rory had this dream: "I was at school and I was in pajamas. I felt nervous, but then I felt pretty good. But not as good as when I'm home in my pajamas."

When most people dream of being naked or inappropriately dressed in public (a very common dream), this usually has to do with feeling overexposed. According to Patricia Garfield, a San Francisco-based clinical psychologist who has studied dreams for twenty years, Rory's dream shows that she was feeling somewhat vulnerable at the moment.

"In this situation, she's feeling like things are out of place a little bit, that things may not feel right or that she may be in an awkward situation after the move," says Garfield, author of *Your Child's Dreams* (Ballantine, 1984) and *Women's Bodies, Women's Dreams* (Ballantine, 1989).

If your child has a dream of this nature, you might try saying something along these lines: "A lot of people have that dream. I have it myself sometimes. It sure is uncomfortable not being in the right clothes. Is there anything that feeling reminds you of

or makes you feel like? Have you had that feeling sometimes when you're awake?"

It also helps to give your child extra attention and reassurance. For example, if you're about to make a move of some kind, tell him that he'll be able to bring all of his usual things with him.

■ ■

You can help your child feel in control of her dreams by teaching her the concept of "lucid dreaming" or "creative dreaming." A lucid dreamer who dreams something scary can take action, get assistance within the dream, and change the dream's direction.

Some kids pick up lucid dreaming on their own. Dream researcher Patricia Garfield has interviewed children who said that if they didn't like a dream, they just "changed the channel." Other children can be taught these simple techniques:

1. As you fall asleep, say to yourself over and over, "I'm dreaming." Soon you really will be.

2. Choose someone or something to be your dream ally — a parent, a friend, a stuffed animal. (Some children choose religious figures or superheroes, depending on what they've been exposed to and feel comfortable with.)

3. If a monster appears in your dream, confront it with your ally. Ask the monster, "Why are you bothering me?" Insist that the monster tell you.

4. If the monster keeps bothering you, tell yourself, "I don't like this. Now I'm going to wake up." With practice, you'll be able to wake yourself up out of any nightmare.

Here are some concrete ways to encourage your child to share, understand, and take power over his or her dreams.

▶   Start by sharing your own dreams.

▶   Suggest that your child keep a dream journal (see pages 19-20). Besides having an ongoing record of her nighttime adventures, your youngster will often be able to use her dream journal to figure out the meaning of dream series that occur during a particular time of her life.

"When you have them all together in a group, you can see how they relate to each other," says Jonni Kincher, author of *Dreams Can Help: A Journal Guide to Understanding Your Dreams and Making Them Work For You* (Free Spirit Publishing, 1989). "Sometimes you learn what your certain symbol is. When you look back, in light of new dreams, the old ones tend to make a lot more sense."

Kincher advises her students to ask themselves these questions when searching for patterns in their dreams: How many dreams go from good to bad? From bad to good? How many star you as the hero? As the victim? Which images repeat or reappear in disguised form? How did they change? (Examples: Going from big to small, young to old, real to artificial, and so on.)

▶ Your child might benefit from the experience of using clay and other materials to "make" his dreams. Kincher has her workshop students create bumper stickers, cartoons, even limericks that have to do with their dreams. "The more different things you do," she explains, "the more you fool around with one dream, the more things pop out, and the more associations are made."

Dreams can provide inspiration for original art of various kinds. My husband Stephen is a poet who writes every morning as soon as he awakens. His dreams are often rich with poetic imagery, and sometimes he dreams actual lines of poetry.

▶ Patricia Garfield suggests that when your child tells you a dream, you might reply, "That's a wonderful dream. That's really such an interesting picture. I would love to see that. Could you draw it for me?"

"The act of putting it on paper helps resolve even very negative feelings," Garfield says. "There's something about externalizing the imagery that helps the dreamer have a sense of control over it. That would be very helpful in resolving any residual anxiety."

If your child draws a nightmare, pose questions about his picture. Anne Sayre Wiseman, author of *Nightmare Help: A Guide for Parents and Teachers* (Ten Speed Press, 1989), has

come up with questions that can guide a child in finding his or her own solution to a bad dream: What will you do to help the person in the picture? How does it feel to be stuck? How will you make the situation less scary? If your nightmare vision could speak, what would it say? What would you like to tell it? If you could have more power, what would you do to help yourself in the dream?

▶ To help your child better catch and hold a dream, suggest that she make a point of reminding herself to remember a dream just before she goes to bed.

▶ A number of themes are commonly found in children's dreams. Animals with sharp teeth are often associated with dreams of anger. Frustration in trying to do something often indicates difficulty in communicating. Sensing something terrifying or dangerous may mean the child feels insecure or threatened.

Can your child remember and interpret any of his own dream themes?

PHYSIOLOGICAL PSYCHOLOGY: EXPLORING THE SENSES

A few easy experiments will give your child some idea of the workings of her own senses, another area psychologists study.

▶ An optical illusion is a mistake your brain makes in judging the color, shape, size, or distance of an object.

With your right hand, hold an empty toilet paper tube (or a sheet of paper rolled into a tube with a one-inch opening) in front of your right eye. With your left hand, touch the left side of the tube about six inches from your face. Your palm should be facing toward you, your fingers held together and pointing upward.

Keeping both eyes open, look through the tube at the wall across the room. You'll see a "hole" in the palm of your hand.

The reason? While we normally see a composite of the images received by both eyes, here only the right eye can see

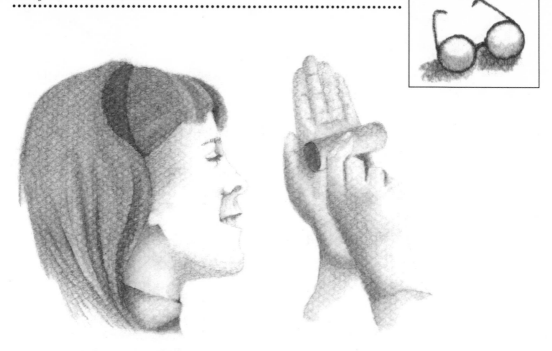

the hole at the end of the tube, and only the left eye can see your hand holding the tube. Since both images are directly ahead, they overlap to cause the illusion.

▶ Are you right-eyed or left-eyed? Find out by extending one arm and pointing your index finger at some spot across the room. Keep both eyes open. Then close one eye at a time.

You'll see two different views of your pointing finger. If the view you see with your right eye is the same as the one you saw with both eyes, your right eye is the dominant one.

▶ Hold a mirror perpendicular to a piece of paper on a table. Have your child try to write his name or draw a simple square while watching his hand only in the mirror.

▶ Test your child's skin sensitivity. You'll need a pair of dividers (or compasses of the kind used to draw a circle) and a millimeter or inch ruler.

Ask your child to close her eyes and keep them closed during the testing. Set the two points of the dividers 45 millimeters (1 7/8 inches) apart. Lightly touch your child's forearm with the divider. She will probably feel two points. Now change the distance to 35 millimeters (or 1 1/4 inches) and lightly touch her forearm again. This time she may feel only one point.

Try the smaller setting on her cheek. Since the cheek is more sensitive, she will probably feel two points there.

If your child enjoys this exercise, try to determine how sensitive a fingertip is; the back of the hand; the chest; the lips.

▶ You can map your tongue's sensitivity to different kinds of tastes. Try placing each of these on the tip, side, and back of your tongue: a bit of salt (salty), sugar (sweet), lemon juice (sour), and powdered coffee (bitter).

You'll find that the tip of the tongue is more sensitive to salty and sweet tastes, the sides are more sensitive to salty and sour, and the back is more sensitive to bitter.

▶ Find out whether lukewarm feels hot or cold. Fill three pans — one with hot water, one with cold water, and one with lukewarm water (put this one in the middle). Have your child place his left-hand fingertips in the pan on the left side, and his right-hand fingertips in the pan on the right side. After you count to sixty, your child puts both of his hands in the middle (lukewarm) pan. One of his hands will "think" the water is hot, the other will "think" it's cold.

▶ Aphelion, a British perfumer who has designed custom perfumes for royalty and other famous people, is able to distinguish perhaps 2,500 different scents. He uses this unusual ability to capture the unique individual fragrance, or "odor signature," of each of his clients.

Take a "smell walk" around your house or neighborhood and count how many separate scents you and your child can distinguish.

▶ Children enjoy testing their bodies' reaction times. Here are two activities your child can try:

a) Hold your arm out, with the back of your hand up. Put a penny on the back of your hand. Tilt your hand until the penny slides off, and try to catch the penny with the same hand. Keep track of your successes and see if your rate improves with practice.

b) Hold your hand out with the thumb and forefinger separated and ready to catch something. Your other fingers should be curled in. Another person holds a yardstick by the top edge, with the bottom tip between your thumb and forefinger. When he drops it, see how long it takes you to catch it.

▶ A practical ability you can teach your child is how to relax. One of the simplest ways is to tell her first to tense up every muscle in her body, from head to toe, then to slowly relax each muscle and body part, one by one.

■ ■ ■ ■ ■ ■ ■ ■ ■ ■ ■ ■ ■ ■ ■ ■ ■ ■ ■ ■

IS YOUR CHILD A TYPE T?

Several psychologists have come up with questionnaires to determine whether someone is a "sensation-seeker." Another label for this is "Type T" personality (thrill-seeker).

Studies have found that more males than females fall into this category, and that males are more susceptible to boredom. Highest rates for thrill-seeking for both males and females are found in the 16–24 age range, after which they gradually drop off.

It might be fun to find out if your child is a Type T. Here are some activities to try.

▶ Brainstorm with your child some possible thrill-seeking activities. Discuss motivations for seeking thrills, such as excitement, defiance, self-respect, self-discovery, escape. Talk about the difference between the following terms and find examples of each: thrill-seeking, risk-taking, adventure, excitement. Ask these questions and others of your own: What would you do if you had a large sum of money? How are you at waiting? Which do you prefer, old friends or new friends? Are you adventurous about trying new foods? Would you ever try parachuting? How would you describe your dream job?

▶ One of humankind's oldest desires has been to alter consciousness, or to feel "high." The bad news, of course, is that this has led to the abuse of alcohol and other drugs. The good news is that there are actually quite a few ways to alter one's consciousness without using harmful substances.

In *The Book of Highs: 250 Methods for Altering Your Consciousness Without Drugs* (originally published in 1973, now out of print), author Edward Rosenfeld suggested some very unusual ones: Read aloud James Joyce's novel, *Finnegans Wake*. Give yourself the sensation of compressing time (for example, to make an hour seem to pass every five minutes, eat every half hour or so and sleep very briefly). Be aware of death by living every hour as though it were your last.

Work with your child to develop a personal list of ways to feel "high" in healthy ways. Examples suitable to young people include: 1) exercising, which has been shown to raise levels of endorphins (natural mood-boosters), 2) competing in sports and games, which are mentally and physically exciting, 3) listening to music, making music, dancing, 4) laughing, 5) accomplishing something, 6) meditation, which is an age-old method of relaxing the body and focusing the mind.

■ ■

MEMORY MYSTERIES

Steve walked in the door, dropping his keys on the dining room table, his books on the kitchen table on his way to the refrigerator, and his shoes in the living room next to the phone. The next morning Steve spent precious minutes searching for his shoes, books, and keys, and was late for class.

Richard, an artist, had only visited Steve's house once, many months before. Yet he could describe in detail each room's layout, including the fabric and color of each piece of furniture. When he asked Steve to close his eyes and describe what Richard was wearing at that moment, Steve could only venture a guess: "Something blue-ish?"

Share these basic facts about memory with your child:

Memory abilities vary by individual, but the processes of memory work the same in everyone. Depending on how long you want to remember something, your brain stores information in three different ways, or stages.

The first stage is called "sensory register." Usually your eyes hold onto an image for only a fraction of a second before it's replaced by another image.

Sensory memory fades quickly unless it's transferred to the next stage, called "short-term memory" or STM. When Steve dropped his keys on the table, he saw what he was doing but didn't think about it. The image of keys in that particular location never made it into his memory.

STM is an active memory, the part of your mind that holds the contents of your attention. What you choose to keep in STM is a matter of personal interest. It usually decays within 15–20 seconds unless you consciously attend to it.

The third stage, called "long-term memory" or LTM, is practically limitless. It can hold as many as one quadrillion separate bits of information.

The longer you think about something, the longer it stays in STM and the greater its chances of moving to LTM.

Here are some ways to test and strengthen your child's memory abilities.

▶ Both you and your child can do this at the same time: Try to draw from memory as many details as possible of what's on each side of a U.S. penny (or another common coin).

Most people can only recall a few of the penny's features. Though we handle pennies nearly every day of our lives, their details are not significant enough for us to commit them to memory.

▶ Fill a tray with ten to twenty small, common, related items — baby care products, kitchen utensils, assorted pieces of hardware. Show the tray to your child for one minute, then put it out of sight. Ask your child how many items she can recall. (Either she can write them down, or you can write them down as she calls them out to you.) Afterward, check the tray to find out how many items she named correctly.

Many people who try this activity don't do very well. With practice and a few tricks, however, the memory can be improved.

Fill a tray again, and this time suggest to your child that she think through the way the items are used, placing them in some sort of order in her mind. She'll have to think very quickly.

Example: "First you open the diaper pin, take off the baby's diaper, then apply baby powder, while holding a rattle to distract the baby, then you wash your hands with the soap, then dry them on a bib, then feed the baby using the spoon," and so on.

Your child's performance should be much improved, partly due to the effort of focusing her mind.

▶ Teach your child the "Method of Loci," a way to commit a list of unrelated items to memory. Basically, you link the items you want to remember with familiar locations, following a predetermined order (such as clockwise).

Example: Imagine each item on the list as being in a particular spot within a room. The glass is on the shelf as you enter, the broom stands next to the shelf, the book is on the record player, and so on. Mentally take a trip around the room to visit each item.

Once you've explained the Method of Loci, give your child a list of unrelated household items to commit to memory.

▶ Teach your child how to make associations.

Example: When you meet a new person and want to remember his or her name, think up something funny or bizarre to associate with it. Say your son wants to remember

the name of his new coach, Jimmy Ruder. He might associate his coach with the phrase, "He's ruder than the old coach."

▶ Practice making use of mnemonics (from the Greek *mneme*, to remember). A mnemonic is any technique that helps you remember things better, usually by forming a strong association. It could be anything from a rhyme ("Thirty days hath September...") to a strong visual image to putting a rubber band on your wrist.

▶ Tell your child about *déjà vu*: that feeling we all get sometimes that we've been in a particular place or situation before, even though we know that's impossible. Scientists don't know for sure why this is such a common experience, but several theories have been suggested. Perhaps a situation feels familiar because it triggers memories of an experience that evoked similar feelings. Or maybe it has something to do with a slight lag time between the processing mechanisms of two parts of the brain.

Has your child ever experienced *déjà vu?*

PSYCHOLOGY PURSUITS

▶ Experiment with time awareness. Hold a watch and ask your child to sit quietly and let you know when she thinks one minute has gone by; five minutes; ten minutes.

Find out how her accuracy is affected when you ask her to gauge the same amounts of time while engaged in some interesting activity. (Why is it said that a watched pot never boils?)

▶ Here's an experiment psychologists have used to demonstrate that each half of the brain draws on reserves to allow people to pay attention.

Have your child sit at a table and tap his right index finger steadily. Now ask him to start talking to you. As he speaks, his tapping will slow.

Ask him to switch hands, tapping with his left index finger while speaking aloud. His tapping won't slow.

Why? Because both the right hand and the speech function are controlled by the brain's left hemisphere. Using both at once drains attention from the same side of the brain.

Most (but not all) left-handers have the same left-hemisphere dominance for language as righties. Try this experiment on several righties and lefties and compare results.

▶ The Rorschach test uses cards printed with what look like inkblots. You look at the blots and tell what you "see" in them.

Psychologists and psychiatrists use the Rorschach to analyze a client's mental state. It takes much training to be able to understand and make use of the responses.

Have your child make her own "inkblot" cards, following these simple steps: 1) Drip some paint or ink in the center of a piece of paper. 2) Fold the paper exactly in half, lay it on a table, and press down on it so the paint spreads out in a random pattern. 3) Open and let dry. 4) Repeat until you have as many inkblots as you want.

Ask family and friends to take turns telling what they see in the blots. Aim for creative responses and the fun of the unexpected, without bothering about the deeper meanings of what each person sees.

▶ To enhance your youngster's ability to express feelings and articulate emotions, work with him to enrich his vocabulary of feeling words.

List words describing various feeling states and go over them with your child. (The "How Do You Feel Today?" poster can help with this activity; see Resources, page 184.) Talk about the kinds of situations which might lead to each of the different emotions. (*Stick Up For Yourself! Every Kid's Guide to Personal Power and Positive Self-Esteem* by Gershen Kaufman, Ph.D. and Lev Raphael, Ph.D. treats this at some length; see Resources, page 185.) Try to figure out what is common to all the times your child feels a certain way, such as fearful.

Examples: You think something bad is about to happen; you expect that you won't get your needs met; you don't know how to deal with a problem.

With a young child, stick to the more basic emotions —happy, sad, angry, afraid — and have him act them out. Or he can draw, sing, or dance them.

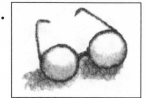

▶ Just for fun, introduce the concept of psychic abilities and extrasensory perception (ESP).

Hold a deck of cards and turn them over one at a time while your child guesses what the next card will be. (You could limit the guesses to "red" or "black" to improve her chances.) Then switch so she turns the cards and you do the guessing. Keep track of correct guesses.

▶ If there's a psychologist or family therapist among your acquaintances, see if it's possible for your child to "interview" him or her. Some questions he might ask are: Do you work with individuals or groups? Do you give psychological tests? Do you train other people to work as counselors? Do you teach or do research? How do you learn about someone's personality, abilities, and behaviors?

What kinds of questions do you ask people? Do you tell them what you think of their answers? What kinds of routine tasks do you do every day? How do you get people to come to you for counseling?

▶ The next time you're in a supermarket, department store, or bank with your older child, pay attention to the psychological dynamics of the people around you. Later on, talk about what you saw.

Who was bossing someone else around? Who was being bossed? Was one person being critical of another? Did people seem to play different roles with their families and friends, compared to the way they behaved with customers or store employees?

▶ Constant grumblers aren't much fun to be with. But most people enjoy spending time with people who can look on the bright side of almost any situation.

You can help your child to become someone who isn't thrown by life's little inconveniences and has a generally bright personal outlook.

Example: Have a "Positive Week." Every time a negative thought enters your mind, turn it around to a positive one.

The first day I tried this, it rained on my daily walk. Normally, these would have been my thoughts: "My hair is going to flop, my tennis shoes will take hours to dry, I'm

going to have to change my clothes when I get home." But during my "positive week," my thoughts went like this instead: "This rain is wonderful, flowers will grow, people won't have to water their lawns, the air feels cleaner, and I'm experiencing nature in a gentle way." And I actually felt good.

■ ■ ■ ■ ■ ■ ■ ■ ■ ■ ■ ■ ■ ■ ■ ■ ■ ■ ■

SPECIAL EFFECTS

Find ways for you and your child to demonstrate these "special effects," each of which has important implications in psychology.

1. **The Hawthorne Effect.** When researchers at a factory in Hawthorne, Illinois, studied how light affects workers, they found that no matter how the lighting was changed, the workers were always more productive than they were before the change.

Just knowing that someone is watching seems to change people's behavior. Think of situations when you or your child were being watched. How did this affect your behavior?

When your child was a toddler, were you more patient with his demands in the supermarket if you knew you were being observed by other shoppers? When your child takes a test, are the results better or worse than when he performs the exact same work unobserved?

2. *The Placebo Effect.* It's been shown many times that a pill containing no active ingredients, only sugar, will have some effect on a person's medical complaint. It can even have as much effect as a pill containing actual medication. All that's necessary is for the person taking the pill to believe there's something helpful in it.

At home, you can see the Placebo Effect in action in the way a mother's kiss has remarkable healing powers, or when a child feels better after putting a Band-Aid on a cut. Can you and your child think of other examples of this?

3. *The Rosenthal Effect.* Also called the Pygmalion Effect or the "self-fulfilling prophecy." Many experiments have shown that experimenter's expectations can powerfully affect the results.

Example: In a famous study, teachers were told that one group of students had scored high on a test for intellectual blooming while a second group had scored "average." The teachers saw the first group as happier, more interesting, and more curious than the second group, when in fact the two groups were no different.

The study also showed that the "smarter" children, on average, gained more points when retested than their classmates.

Teach your child a difficult new task. Act as if you assume she'll learn it easily. What happens?

■ ■

RESOURCES

The Centering Book: Awareness Activities for Children and Adults to Relax the Body and Mind by Gay Hendricks and Russel Wills (Prentice Hall, 1989) and *The Second Centering Book* by Gay Hendricks and Thomas B. Roberts (Prentice Hall, 1989). These books teach centering and awareness techniques to help children relax and get in touch with their creativity. The first book covers yoga, relaxation training, imagery, and working with dreams, while the sequel delves into fantasy, meditation, intuition, and feelings.

"How Do You Feel Today?" Part I and Part II. Two 16" x 24" posters, each playfully illustrating 35 different emotions (aggressive, disbelieving, hurt, paranoid, smug, withdrawn, and so on). Therapists and teachers use them to open up communication with children about feelings, but they're also excellent tools for vocabulary building at home. Available in regular or laminated versions. (The company also offers a poster called "How Does Your Cat Feel Today?") Write: How Do You Feel Today? Productions, P. O. Box 1085, Agoura, California 91301. Or call (818) 706-2288 or (818) 990-6782.

It's All In Your Head: A Guide to Understanding Your Brain and Boosting Your Brain Power by Susan L. Barrett (Free Spirit Publishing, 1985). For ages 9–15. Explains how you think, learn, and remember, and how to be more creative. Explores what genius is, whether you can learn in your sleep, and whether there's anything to ESP.

Liking Myself: Assertiveness Training for Ages 5–9 by Pat Palmer, Ed.D. (Impact Publishers, 1986). This small book introduces young children to the important concepts of self-esteem and talking about feelings.

The Mouse, the Monster and Me: Assertiveness Training for Ages 8–12 by Pat Palmer, Ed.D. (Impact Publishers, 1984). Children are taught how to find the power within themselves to get their needs met, how to say no, and how to deal with criticism and compliments.

On Monday When It Rained by Cherryl Kachenmeister, photographs by Tom Berthiaume (Houghton Mifflin, 1989). Using text and expressive photographs, this simple book describes a variety of situations and the resulting emotions felt by a young boy, including embarrassment, pride, excitement, and anger.

Pileup Game by Nancy Loving Tubesing, Ed.D., and Donald A. Tubesing, Ph.D. For ages 10 and up. In this unusual game, players learn to cope creatively with multiple stressors. Self-discovery, not winning, is the object of the main game and a dozen alternatives outlined in the accompanying activity booklet. For example, if bad weather hurts the family business (a financial stressor), would you procrastinate, use food to console yourself, or fret (all negative coping mechanisms), or would you discuss the problem, get organized, and set priorities (positive possibilities)? Write: Whole Person Press, P.O. Box 3151, Duluth, Minnesota 55803.

Psychology for Kids: 40 Fun Tests that Help You Learn About Yourself by Jonni Kincher (Free Spirit Publishing, Inc., 1990). For ages 10 and up. Are you an extrovert or an introvert? An optimist or a pessimist? Are you creative? What body language do you speak? The tests in this book take the mystery out of psychology and empower children to learn more about themselves. Based on psychological theories and research, "field tested" with children.

Stick Up For Yourself! Every Kid's Guide to Personal Power and Positive Self-Esteem by Gershen Kaufman, Ph.D., and Lev Raphael, Ph.D. (Free Spirit Publishing, Inc., 1990). For ages 8–12. This book shows young people how to make choices, be healthily assertive about their needs, and feel better about themselves. It includes a sizable section on developing a feelings vocabulary.

T.A. for Kids and Grown-Ups, Too: How to Feel OK About Yourself and Other People by Alvyn and Margaret Freed (Jalmar Press, 1977). Also by Dr. Freed: *T.A. for Tots and T.A. for Teens.* These are juvenile versions of Transactional Analysis (TA), which is based on the theory of parent, adult, and child ego states.

Introducing Famous Authors Through Their Books for Children

You can expose your children to first-rate reading by introducing them to children's books written by famous authors of adult works. When you choose stories and poems for children by celebrated writers, you know at the outset that they write well. Since their tales and verses were usually first loved by their own youngsters, other young readers are likely to find them appealing. These authors have learned the knack of not talking down to their audience.

Like all the best children's literature, the books described in this section are also stimulating to adult readers. An excellent example is poet Randall Jarrell's *The Bat-Poet* (Macmillan, 1963), a beautifully written and touching allegory for ages eight and up.

This sensitive story of a poetry-writing bat who can't sleep during the days works on more than one level. When the bat-poet's peers make fun of his creative images, he doesn't stop making up poems — he just stops sharing them with his fellow bats. He fares little better with a mockingbird, who, though he admires the bat's poem, analyzes its rhyme scheme instead of feeling its emotion. When the bat-poet does find an appreciative audience, he is able to unleash more of his imagination. Young readers will come away with a positive feeling about being true to one's nature, as well as an increased appreciation for poetic imagery and the difficulties of the artist's life.

John Gardner, known for such brilliant novels as *Grendel, The Sunlight Dialogues,* and *Nickel Mountain,* wrote several books of fairy tales which wildly and hilariously deviate from the usual. In *Dragon, Dragon, and Other Tales* (Alfred A. Knopf, 1975), a dragon terrorizes the kingdom by stealing spark plugs from people's cars, among other irritating behaviors. A cobbler's son disguises himself as a brush salesman in order to confront the dragon. In *Gudgekin the Thistle Girl* (Knopf, 1976), Gardner irreverently parodies the entire genre and invents a princess with spunk. Other books by Gardner to look for: *A Child's Bestiary* and *The King of the Hummingbirds* (both Knopf, 1977).

There are at least two more good reasons to track down many of the books listed here. These brief works are a fine way for your child to get to know prominent authors without the difficulty of tackling full-length adult works. And later in life, when he or she is required to read the longer, more advanced novels and poems in high school or college classes, they won't seem so intimidating because your child will be meeting old friends.

CHILDREN'S BOOKS BY FAMOUS AUTHORS: RECOMMENDED READINGS

Many of the newer books described here may be found in book-stores and larger libraries. The older and out-of-print ones might take some detective work. Start by checking the current edition of *Books in Print* or *Children's Books in Print* at any library or bookstore. While you're consulting these reference works, you can also look up any of your favorite authors and determine if they have written children's books.

For out-of-print books, visit libraries and secondhand bookstores.

Barthelme, Donald, *The Slightly Irregular Fire Engine* (Farrar, Straus & Giroux, 1971). For ages 5–11. In 1887, a plucky little girl investigates a mysterious Chinese house that suddenly appears in her back yard. Her escapades are illustrated by nineteenth-century engravings.

Beattie, Ann, *Spectacles* (Ariel/Workman, 1985). For ages 8–12. When an eight-year-old girl puts on her grumpy great-grand-mother's glasses, they become magical and enable her to see into the past. She begins to understand some of the older woman's frustrations.

Buckley, William F., Jr., *The Temptation of Wilfred Malachey* (Workman, 1985). For ages 8–13. This modern morality tale is about an IBM mainframe computer which teaches a prep-school student that computing can be more profitable than petty theft.

Capote, Truman, *A Christmas Memory* (Alfred A. Knopf, 1989). Capote's heartwarming memoir, packaged in this edition with an audiotape of the story narrated by Celeste Holm, recounts his own childhood in a rural Alabama household of the 1930s.

Ciardi, John, *The Hopeful Trout and Other Limericks* (Houghton Mifflin, 1989). Ciardi was a poet and an author of books about poetry. This volume for children contains 40 preposterous limericks.

More Ciardi for children: *I Met a Man, Fast and Slow,* and *Doodle Soup.*

189

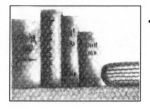

Clavell, James, *Thrump-O-Moto* (Delacorte, 1986). For ages 5 and up. The author of *Shogun* and other blockbuster Asian sagas has here produced a complicated fantasy about a Japanese apprentice wizard who travels through time-space folds.

cummings, e.e., *Fairy Tales* (Harcourt Brace Jovanovich, 1978). For ages 4–8. These four humorous and imaginative tales, written by poet cummings for his own small daughter, have titles like "The House That Ate Mosquito Pie" and "The Little Girl Named I."

Dickey, James, *Bronwen, the Traw, and the Shape-Shifter: A Poem in Four Parts* (Harcourt Brace Jovanovich, 1986). For ages 5–10. The poet and novelist (*Deliverance*) wrote this poem based on stories he told his daughter Bronwen when she was three and four. It's long (122 stanzas), though the language is lyrical.

Eco, Umberto, *The Bomb and the General* and *The Three Astronauts* (Harcourt Brace Jovanovich, both 1989). For ages 4–8. Eco, Italian author of the best-selling *The Name of the Rose* and *Foucault's Pendulum,* has written two simple stories. The first is a scary (and oversimplified) plea for world peace, in which the atoms decide to vacate bombs so they fall harmlessly, putting a war-mongering general in his place (as a doorman). The second supports intercultural understanding and harmony: An American, Russian, and Chinese make friends with one another and a Martian, once they realize that each of them is capable of loneliness and tears. Both volumes are colorfully and artistically illustrated by Eugenio Carmi.

Eliot, T.S., *Old Possum's Book of Practical Cats,* illustrated by Edward Gorey (Harcourt Brace Jovanovich, 1982). For all ages. This book became more widely known due to the long-running play, *Cats.* Reading aloud these appealing rhymes about the personalities and antics of particular cats could lead to an appreciation of Eliot and poetry, along with introducing some interesting new vocabulary.
   Growltiger's Last Stand and Other Poems (Farrar, Straus & Giroux, 1990) is a picture book containing three poems from *Old Possum's Book of Practical Cats.*

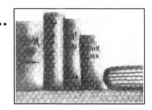

Fast, Howard, *The Magic Door* (Peace Press, 1952). For ages 10–14. The author of *Spartacus* and *Freedom Road* wrote this book about a boy in a 1920s New York City tenement who passes through a door into a lush past world.

Fleming, Ian, *Chitty Chitty Bang Bang* (Alfred A. Knopf, 1989). For ages 8 and up. The creator of the James Bond thrillers concocted a witty adventure about a magical car that confronts Joe the Monster. Lots of nice touches.

Frost, Robert, *You Come Too: Favorite Poems for Young Readers* (Henry Holt, 1975). In 1959, when the famous poet was 85, he gathered these poems as especially suitable for young people. Not surprisingly, many of them have to do with nature, at least on the surface, including "The Road Not Taken."

Hall, Donald, *The Man Who Lived Alone* (David R. Godine, 1984). For ages 5–9. This is the simply told life story of a self-sufficient man who chooses to live alone.

Hall, a poet, also wrote *The Ox-Cart Man* (Viking, 1980) which won the Caldecott Medal.

Helprin, Mark, *Swan Lake* (Houghton Mifflin, 1989). Illustrated by Chris Van Allsburg. For ages 7 and up. The author of *Winter's Tale* and other works has created an elaborate narrative as a background for the characters in the ballet "Swan Lake."

Herriot, James, *Only One Woof* (St. Martin's Press, 1985). For ages 6 and up. A silent sheepdog accompanies his master at his chores, never barking until he sees his brother for the first time since they were separated as pups.

More Herriot tales suitable for children: *Moses the Kitten* and *The Christmas Day Kitten*.

Hoban, Russell, *How Tom Beat Captain Najork and His Hired Sportsmen* (Puffin/Penguin, 1978). For ages 5 and up. Young readers delight in the understated British humor of this story by the author of *Riddley Walker* and *Turtle Diary*. A strong point is made for the value of fooling around as an aid to creativity.

— *The Flight of Bembel Rudzuk* (Putnam, 1982). In this funny picture book for ages 4–7, wizard Bembel Rudzuk (our young hero) creates a "squidgerino squelcher" (using three jars of monster powder), which annoys the princess (actually Mother, who wonders who is going to clean up the mess).

— *The Marzipan Pig* (Farrar, Straus & Giroux, 1986). A delightful, touching story that begins with a marzipan pig who gathers dust behind the sofa until eaten by a mouse. The mouse then falls in love with an unresponsive clock, and an owl falls in love with a taxi meter, and a hibiscus tries hard not to die.

Yet another Hoban book worth reading: *Harvey's Hideout.*

Huxley, Aldous, *The Crows of Pearblossom* (Random House, 1967). For ages 4 and up. In 1944, the famous English novelist wrote his only children's book for his young niece. In this simple and amusing tale, a hungry snake keeps eating Mrs. Crow's newly laid eggs, until Mr. Crow and his friend Old Man Owl fool the snake into eating some disguised clay eggs. Unfortunately, Mrs. Crow isn't treated very respectfully by her husband, and is described as rather helpless. Huxley was, of course, a product of his culture, and parent-child discussion of such stereotyping is appropriate.

Ionesco, Eugene, *Story Number 3* (Harlin Quist, 1971). For ages 3–5. In this simple and magical tale by the celebrated playwright, little Josette visits her Papa in bed one morning and asks for a story. They then take an imaginary plane ride above the city.

In *Story Number 1* and *Story Number 2,* for children under 3, we are first introduced to Josette, and in *Story Number 4,* Josette plays hide-and-seek with her Papa.

Jarrell, Randall, *The Animal Family* (Alfred A. Knopf, Inc., 1965). For ages 8 and up. Illustrated by Maurice Sendak. I put this seven-chapter book down briefly, and then only to prolong the pleasure it gave me. Jarrell's last work before his death, a Newbery Honor Book, is a moving fantasy of how a solitary man finds a family — a mermaid, bear, lynx, and finally a little boy. The language is poetic (Jarrell doesn't hesitate occasionally to use words that would never appear in a basal reader). The characters are kind and understanding toward each other, even when their respective species and cultures are impossibly different.

— *Snow-White and the Seven Dwarfs* (Farrar, Straus & Giroux, 1987). For ages 5 and up. This version was translated beautifully by Jarrell, who said he tried to make it as much like the original German story as he could. Nancy Ekholm Burkert's illustrations won the Caldecott medal.

Jarrell also wrote *The Gingerbread Rabbit* (1964) and *Fly by Night* (1976).

Joyce, James, *The Cat and the Devil* (Schocken, 1981). For ages 6 and up. This simple story is actually a letter Joyce wrote to his grandson Stephen in 1936. (A crucial few lines are in French.)

Kazantzakis, Nikos, *At the Palaces of Knossos* (Ohio University Press, 1988). For ages 12 and up. The author of *Zorba the Greek* and *The Last Temptation of Christ* originally wrote this adventure story for an Athenian youth periodical. Its characters are those of classical Greek mythology, and a historical chronology at the end helps readers put events into perspective.

Keneally, Thomas, *Ned Kelly and the City of the Bees* (David R. Godine, 1981). For ages 7–12. The Australian author of *Schindler's List* and many other novels wrote this first-person inside-a-beehive adventure for his daughters.

Kennedy, William, and Brendan Kennedy, *Charlie Malarkey and the Belly Button Machine* (Atlantic Monthly Press, 1986). For ages 4–8. The Pulitzer Prize-winning author (*Ironweed*) began co-writing this amusing bedtime story with his son when Brendan was four.

King, Stephen, *The Eyes of the Dragon* (Viking, 1987). For ages 8 and up. King wrote this adventure/fantasy/fairy tale for his thirteen-year-old daughter because she had no interest in his popular horror stories. The simply written full-length book, complete with dragons, princes, and magic, has a read-aloud feel.

Klein, A. M., *Doctor Dwarf & Other Poems for Children* (Quarry Press, 1989). For all ages. This volume contains the verses the Canadian poet (1909–1972) wrote for his children. In them he tells the history and recounts the legends of the Jewish tradition.

Koontz, Dean R., *Oddkins: A Fable for All Ages* (Warner, 1988). For ages 5 and up. This 192-page book by the well-known terror and suspense writer leads up to a battle between the Oddkins (good toys that help children who need a friend) and the bad toys. Good read-aloud fun on dark and stormy nights.

Kotzwinkle, William, *Trouble in Bugland: A Collection of Inspector Mantis Mysteries* (David R. Godine, 1986). For ages 10 and up. These are clever and humorous take-offs on the Sherlock Holmes mysteries.
— *Hearts of Wood & Other Timeless Tales* (Godine, 1986). Here the novelist and poet offers five fairy tales about such wonders as carousel horses that come alive and a butterfly catcher who dreams he is a butterfly.

LeGuin, Ursula K., *Catwings* and *Catwings Return* (Orchard Books, 1988 and 1989, respectively). For ages 7–10. For these two books, the award-winning author of fantasies for adults and children chose the premise of four winged kittens who fly away from the dangers of the inner city. The characters, though cats, have realistic histories and human emotions. The endings are warm and satisfying, after the cats experience some interesting adventures.
— *Leese Webster* (Atheneum, 1979). For ages 5–9. This is a simple book about a spider whose elaborately woven pictures become museum pieces.
— *A Visit from Dr. Katz* (Atheneum, 1988). For ages 5–8. A tale about two orange and white cats who help cure their young female owner of the flu by curling up on her tummy.

Mamet, David, *Warm and Cold* (Grove Press, 1989). For ages 4–7. The Pulitzer Prize-winning playwright (*Glengarry Glen Ross*), who also wrote the screenplays for (and directed) *The House of Games* and *Things Change,* collaborated with artist

Donald Sultan on this picture book. It's a very brief and evocative tale of a man traveling by train in winter, away from those he loves.

Mamet also wrote *Three Children's Plays* (Grove, 1986).

Maurois, Andre, *Fattypuffs and Thinifers* (Alfred A. Knopf, 1989). Two boys find themselves on opposite sides of a negotiating table because the nations of the Fattypuffs and the Thinifers want to fight about their differences.

Plath, Sylvia, *The Bed Book* (Harper Junior Books, 1989). Plath wrote this poem for her own children. The bedtimes of four-to-eight-year-olds will be enriched by her imaginative verses about all kinds of odd sleeping places.

Rossetti, Christina, *Goblin Market* (David R. Godine, 1981). For ages 9 and up. Christina was Dante Gabriel Rossetti's sister and a pre-Raphaelite poet who wrote religious verse. This version of *Goblin Market,* which was first published in 1862, features haunting drawings to complement the lilting rhythms, vivid imagery, and rich symbolism of Rossetti's poetry.

Saki, *The Story-Teller* (David R. Godine, 1987). For ages 9 and up. All thirteen of these tales by witty short-story writer Saki are about children. In each case, the youngsters come off better than their petty and predictible elders.

Sandburg, Carl, *Rootabaga Stories, Part One* and *Part Two* (Harcourt Brace Jovanovich, 1988 and 1989, respectively). For ages 5 and up. The language in these stories by the Pulitzer Prize-winning poet and biographer is lyrical, while the characters and story lines are strange and fantastic. They are peopled by such oddities as a broom handle that marries a rag doll, two skyscrapers who whisper together and decide to have a child who turns out to be a train, and a jackrabbit who jumps so high he never comes back. One section is entitled, "Four Stories about the Deep Doom of Dark Doorways" (Sandburg does not limit himself to tales of sweetness and light).

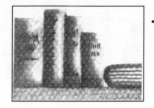

Service, Robert W., *The Shooting of Dan McGrew* (David R. Godine, 1988). This classic read-aloud poem written early in the century by the well-known Canadian poet is set in the time of the Alaskan Gold Rush. Service gained the nickname "Canada's Kipling," and the rhythms in this poem make it easy to see why. The illustrations by Ted Harrison are bold and colorful.

Service and Harrison also worked together on *The Cremation of Sam McGee* (Greenwillow Books, 1987).

Singer, Isaac Bashevis, *Stories for Children* (Farrar, Straus & Giroux, 1985). For all ages. These thirty-six tales by the Nobel Prize-winning author tell about an absent-minded professor who forgets his own address, a Yiddish-speaking parakeet who plays unwitting matchmaker, and a wise rabbi who battles a wicked witch. In simple prose, Singer writes of magic, fools, love, and deceit.

Steel, Danielle, *Max's New Baby, Max and the Baby-sitter, Max's Daddy Goes to the Hospital, Martha's New Daddy, Martha's New School,* and *Martha's Best Friend* (Delacorte, 1989). For ages 4–7. The popular romance author has written these books to help children through some difficult times. Simple language and realistic situations.

Stein, Gertrude, *The World is Round* (North Point Press, 1988). For ages 8 and up. Stein plays with language in this, her only children's book, originally published in 1939. She tells the story of nine-year-old Rose and her search for identity, using idiosyncratic punctuation, verse, and a childlike approach to reality.

Stevenson, Robert Louis, *My Shadow* (David R. Godine, 1989). Glenna Lang's colorful illustrations turn this poem from Stevenson's *A Child's Garden of Verses* into a picture book for two-to-five-year-olds.

Strand, Mark, *Rembrandt Takes a Walk* (Clarkson N. Potter, 1986). Strand, an award-winning poet and author, has written a fantastic and amusing story in which Tom visits his absent-minded art-collecting uncle and finds he can remove food from famous paintings. When Rembrandt steps out of a painting, Tom takes him for a walk around town, where the famous painter is obsessed with drawing everything he sees. Vividly illustrated by artist Red Grooms.

Strand also wrote *The Planet of Lost Things* (1982) and *The Night Book* (1985).

Thomas, Dylan, *A Child's Christmas in Wales* (David R. Godine, 1984). For all ages. First published in 1954, this is probably Thomas's most famous childhood reminiscence. The language is musical and should be read aloud for optimum pleasure.

Thurber, James, *The 13 Clocks* (Simon and Schuster, 1977). For ages 8 and up. A complex and funny fairy story about a warm princess and a wicked duke who is afraid of Now.

Tolkien, J. R. R., *The Hobbit* (Houghton Mifflin, 1989). Forty-eight full-color scenes by Michael Hague enhance this new edition of the popular fantasy of Middle-Earth. Even a seven-year-old might enjoy this lengthy tale if it were read aloud in installments.

— *Smith of Wootton Major* (Houghton Mifflin, 1967). For ages 8 and up. A deftly written fantasy about the odd things that happen to a boy who eats a star at the Feast of Good Children.

Tolkien also wrote *Mr. Bliss* (Houghton Mifflin, 1983) for children.

Tolstoy, Leo, *The Lion and the Puppy and Other Stories for Children* (Seaver Books/Henry Holt, 1988). For ages 5 and up. These twenty-five tales were taken from a primer, published in 1872, which Tolstoy wrote to use with the children in a school he founded. His aim was to invent interesting stories that would teach right from wrong without moralizing, while conveying messages about freedom, courage, generosity, patience, and respect for nature. The title story is about a lion who learns to love a puppy which has been tossed to him for food. When the puppy dies, the lion dies of grief.

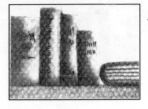

Twain, Mark, *Poor Little Stephen Girard* (Schocken, 1981). For ages 6 and up. A witty short story about a boy who heard of another youth who became successful by collecting pins in front of a bank.

More Twain stories, recently published in Australia and distributed in the U.S. by Publishers Group West, include *A Cat Tale, Legend of Sagenfeld,* and *The Stolen White Elephant.*

Updike, John, *A Child's Calendar* (Knopf, 1965). This series of simple, rhymed poems about the months is suitable for ages four and up.

The Pulitzer Prize-winning author also wrote *The Magic Flute* (1962), *The Ring* (1964), and *Bottom's Dream* (1969).

Walker, Alice, *To Hell With Dying* (Harcourt Brace Jovanovich, 1988). For ages 9 and up. Walker, author of *The Color Purple,* wrote this reminiscence as a short story in 1967. Alcoholic old Mr. Sweet is often on the brink of death, and the children who are his friends save him with kisses, tickles, and love. This story is told from an adult perspective and might confuse some children.

Wilbur, Richard, *Loudmouse* (Harcourt Brace Jovanovich, 1982). For ages 6–10. This story by the Pulitzer Prize-winning poet, first published in 1963, tells of a mouse whose family's safety is endangered because he cannot speak softly.

Wilde, Oscar, *The Happy Prince and Other Stories* (J. M. Dent and Sons, 1968). For ages 6 and up. This volume contains nine magical tales first told by Wilde to his own two sons in 1888. In "The Selfish Giant," a giant keeps children out of his garden, and Spring doesn't come until he has a change of heart. In "The Star Child," a proud child learns humility as he wanders through his medieval world. Some of the stories were also published in separate editions.

Wolitzer, Hilma, *Wish You Were Here* (Farrar, Straus & Giroux, 1984). The characters in Wolitzer's latest book for pre-teens are absolutely believable, as are the characters in her others: *Introducing Shirley Braverman* (1975), *Out of Love* (1976), and

Toby Lived Here (1978). She tackles the everyday and the dramatic, and the ordinary which can be traumatic — divorce, death, war, shyness, loneliness — with skill, humor, and insight. Her adult books include *In the Palomar Arms* and *Silver.*

Woolf, Virginia, *The Widow and the Parrot* (Harcourt Brace Jovanovich, 1988). This story, illustrated by Woolf's grandnephew, was written on request of her nephews, Quentin and Julian Bell, for a family newspaper they put out regularly when they were about twelve years old. They didn't like it; it wasn't as frivolous as they had hoped.

● ● ● ● ●

In addition to the books discussed above, you won't want to deprive your child of the pleasures of Antoine de Saint-Exupéry's *The Little Prince* or E.B. White's classics, *Stuart Little* and *Charlotte's Web.*

The following respected authors have also written children's books:

▶ Margaret Atwood, *Up in the Tree* (1978) and *Anna's Pet* (1980)

▶ William Faulker, *The Wishing Tree*

▶ Rumer Godden, 21 books for children

▶ Ted Hughes, many children's books, including *What Is the Truth?, How the Whale Became,* and *The Iron Giant: A Story in Five Nights*

▶ Maxine Kumin, 17 books for children plus four children's books together with poet Anne Sexton

▶ Alison Lurie, *Clever Gretchen & Other Forgotten Folk Tales, The Heavenly Zoo, Fabulous Beasts*

▶ Theodore Roethke, *Party at the Zoo*

▶ George Sand, *The Mysterious Tale of Gentle Jack and Lord Bumblebee*

▶ May Sarton, *A Walk Through the Woods*

▶ Muriel Spark, *The Very Fine Clock*

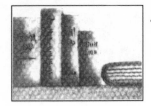

▶ Jean Stafford, *Elephi: The Cat with a High I.Q.*

▶ May Swenson, *Poems to Solve* and *More Poems to Solve*

▶ Voltaire, *The Dog and the Horse*

Salman Rushdie reported that he was working on a fable for children (as of this writing).

One more resource of note: *The Open Door: When Writers First Learned to Read,* selected by Steven Gelbar (David R. Godine, 1989). Gelbar chose excerpts from the works of twenty-nine fascinating writers who discuss how they first became excited by reading and literature. Included are inspiring thoughts from Charles Dickens, Rudyard Kipling, W. B. Yeats, Gertrude Stein, A. A. Milne, Eudora Welty, Annie Dillard, Stephen King, and others.

Selected List of Publishers

Adama Books
306 W. 38th Street
New York, NY 10018
(212) 594-5770

The Book Publishing Co.
P.O. Box 99
Summertown, TN 38483
(615) 964-3571

R.R. Bowker
245 W. 17th St.
New York, NY 10011
1-800-521-8110
In New York, Hawaii, or
Arkansas:
(212) 337-6934 (collect)

Center for Science in
the Public Interest
1501 16th Street, NW
Washington, DC 20036
(202) 332-9110

Chelsea Green Publishing Co.
Route 113
P.O. Box 130
Post Mills, VT 05058-0130
1-800-445-6638
(802) 333-9073

Davis Publications Inc.
50 Portland St.
Worcester, MA 01608
1-800-533-2847
In Massachusetts:
(508) 754-7201

Dawn Publications
14618 Tyler Foot Rd.
Nevada City, CA 95959
1-800-545-7475
In California: (916) 292-3482

Delacorte Press
666 5th Ave.
New York, NY 10103
1-800-223-6834
In New York: (212) 765-6500

Dover Publications
31 E. 2nd St.
Mineola, NY 11501-3582
(516) 294-7000

Earth Works Press
Box 25
1400 Shattuck Ave.
Berkeley, CA 94709
(415) 527-5811

Facts on File
460 Park Ave. So.
New York, NY 10016
(212) 683-2244

Free Spirit Publishing Inc.
400 First Avenue North, Ste. 616
Minneapolis, MN 55401
1-800-735-READ
(612) 338-2068

David R. Godine, Publishers Inc.
300 Massachusetts Ave.
Boston, MA 02115
(617) 536-0761

Grove Press
841 Broadway
New York, NY 10003
1-800-638-6460
(212) 529-3600

Impact Publishers
P.O. Box 1094
San Luis Obispo, CA 93406
(805) 543-5911

Jalmar Press
45 Hitching Post Dr., Bldg. 2
Rolling Hills Estates, CA
90274-4297
1-800-662-9662
(213) 547-1240

Klutz Press
2121 Staunton Ct.
Palo Alto, CA 94306
(415) 424-0739

Lerner Publications Co.
241 First Avenue North
Minneapolis, MN 55401
1-800-328-4929

Lowell House
1875 Century Park East, Ste. 220
Los Angeles, CA 90067
(213) 203-8407

Meadowbrook Press
18318 Minnetonka Blvd.
Deephaven, MN 55391
1-800-338-2232

New Chapter Press
381 Park Ave. South, Ste. 1122
New York, NY 10016
(212) 683-4090

North Point Press
850 Talbot Ave.
Berkeley, CA 94706
(415) 527-6260

Orchard Books/Franklin Watts
387 Park Ave. South
New York, NY 10016
1-800-843-3749
(212) 686-7070

Pond Press
7 Halifax St.
Jamaica Plain, MA 02130
(617) 522-5486

Price, Stern, Sloan
360 N. La Cenega Blvd.
Los Angeles, CA 90048
1-800-421-0892
In California: 1-800-227-8801
(213) 657-6100

Quarry Press
P.O. Box 348
Clayton, NY 13624
or P.O. Box 1061
Kingston, Ontario K7L 4Y5
(613) 548-8429

Running Press
125 S. Twenty-second St.
Philadelphia, PA 19103
1-800-428-1111

Scholastic Inc.
730 Broadway
New York, NY 10003
(212) 505-3000

Shambala Publications
P.O. Box 308, Back Bay Annex
Boston, MA 02117
1-800-444-6514
(617) 424-0030

Sterling Publishing Co.
387 Park Ave. South
New York, NY 10016
1-800-367-9692
In New York: (212) 532-7160

Storey Communications
Pownal, VT 05261
1-800-441-5700
(802) 823-5811

Ten Speed Press/Celestial Arts
P.O. Box 7123
Berkeley, CA 94707
(415) 845-8414

Walker and Company
720 Fifth Ave.
New York, NY 10019
(212) 265-3632

Warren Publishing House, Inc.
17909 Bothell Way SE, #101
Bothell, WA 98012
(206) 485-3335

Williamson Publishing
Charlotte, VT 05445
1-800-234-8791
(802) 425-2102

Writer's Digest Books
1507 Dana Ave.
Cincinnati, OH 45207
1-800-289-0963

Index

A

Abbott, E. A., 43
Absolutely Mad Inventions, 46
Activities diary, 20-21
Additives in food, 131-132
Adulthood, cultural aspects of, 140
The Adventurous Gardener, 114, 117
Advertising slogan, 5
Airports, attending with children, 51
Alcott, Louisa May, 18, 28
Alibis, as creative thinking, 35-39
All I Really Need to Know I Learned in Kindergarten, 42
"All on One Side" game, 85
Amazing Frauds and Astonishing Feats game, 39-40
American Epitaphs, Grave and Humorous, 63
American Sports Poems, 97
America On Display: A Guide to Unusual Museums and Collections in the United States and Canada, 53, 54
The Animal Family, 192-193
Animal shelters, attending with children, 51
Animal shows, 52
Animal Town Game Company catalog, 97
Antique shops, attending with children, 51
Aphelion, 174
Apple trees, growing tips for, 108
Arboretums, 115
Archie McPhee mail-order catalog, 38
Art
  cooking and, 124-125
  dream analysis with, 171
Art from Many Lands, 160
Artisans, visits to, 52
Art Synectics: Stimulating Creativity in Art, 46
Arts, cultural attitudes toward, 146-148
Association games, for memory improvement, 178-179
At the Palaces of Knossos, 193
Atwood, Margaret, 199
Auctions, attending with children, 50
Auto-focus cameras, 67

B

Babar Learns to Cook, 133
Back to the Future, 33
Balloons, games with, 39
Basketball, 89, 91, 93
  science and, 96
The Bat-Poet, 188
Bean seed growing project, 110-111
Beattie, Dennis, 44
The Bed Book, 195
Beliefs. *See* Religious beliefs
Bellamy, Edward, 43
Berawan tribal death customs, 140-141
Bernstein, Leonard, 146-147
Best-Loved Folk-Tales of the World, 160
Best of Gravestone Humor, 63
The Big Book of Kids' List, 13, 44
Billiards, 89-90
Bird-watching, 94
Blood and Guts: A Working Guide to Your Own Insides, 98
Board games, creative rule changing for, 87
Boat rides, 51
Body-brain workouts, 90-94
Body language, cultural differences in, 142-144
The Bomb and the General, 190
"Book of changes" project, 76
The Book of Highs: 250 Methods for Altering Your Consciousness Without Drugs, 176
"Book of Kitsch" project, 38
Books for children, 188-200
  See also Publishers' list and resource list at end of each chapter
Books of Lists, 44
Botanical gardens, 115
Bowling, 88
The Boy From Over There, 160
Brain-benders, 42-44
Brainstorming techniques
  cooking and, 125
  creativity and, xii-xiii
  paper-and-pencil quickies, 9
  photographic projects, 73-74

questions, alibis and mind stretchers for, 35-39
"Type T" personality testing, 175-176
Brancazio, Peter J., 96
Bread, international types of, 126-127
Bronwen, the Traw, and the Shape-Shifter: A Poem in Four Parts, 190
"Brussels sprouts" tag game, 84-85
Bulbs, gardening with, 107

C

Camera equipment, 66-67
Campbell, Joseph, 150-151, 163
Candyland (board game), 87
Card games, creative rule changes for, 88
Carrot Seed, 114, 117
Cartoon collection, 40
The Cat and the Devil, 193
Cats, 95
"Cat's Cradle," 158
Catwings, 194
Catwings Return, 194
Cemetery visits, 55-63
The Centering Book: Awareness Activities for Children and Adults to Relax the Body and Mind, 183
Chang's Paper Pony, 160
Charlie Brown's Fourth Super Book of Questions and Answers About All Kinds of People and How They Live, 139, 160
Charlie Malarkey and the Belly Button Machine, 193
Charlotte's Web, 199
Checkers, 87
Chemistry of food, 132
Chess, 87
Children's Gardens, 117
Children Solve Problems, 42-43
A Child's Bestiary, 188
A Child's Calendar, 198
A Child's Christmas in Wales, 197
"A Child's Garden," 117
Chinese checkers, 87
Chinese New Year, 156
Chitty Chitty Bang Bang, 191
Chopsticks, learning to use, 129
Choron, Sandra, 44

A Christmas Memory, 189
Cinco de Mayo, 157
Cities and towns, historical tours of, 52
Classes, visits to, 52
Climate, cultural diversity and, 139
Clothing, cultural diversity in, 139
Coin shows or shops, 51
Collectibles, photographing, 74
Common Ground Garden Program
catalog, 117
Common senses game, 11-12
Comparative mythology, 150-151
The Complete Adventures of Peter Rabbit,
113, 118
"The Complete Guide to Gardening by
Mail," 118
*The Complete Time Traveler: A Tourist's
Guide to the Fourth Dimension,* 46
Compost
recipe for, 104-105
scientific projects with, 112-113
Computers
cooking and, 127
tours of, 52
"Connections" game, 3
Consciousness altering techniques,
175-176
Container gardening, 103
Conversational habits
cultural differences in, 143-144
physical distance and, 143
Cookbooks
child-produced, 130
for children, 122-123, 134-135
ethnic foods in, 139
Cooking
with children, 121-135
classes for children, 129-130
educational aspects of, 124-127
ethnic dishes, 128
Cooking the Russian Way, etc. (ethnic
cooking series), 133
Cooperative game playing, 84-86
The Cooperative Sports and Games Books,
98
"Coretta Scott King Award and Honor
Books," 160
Courage Children's Illustrated World Atlas,
160
Courtroom sessions, visits to, 52
Creation myths, 151

Creative Food Experiences for Children,
127, 131, 133
Creative game changing, 86-90
*The Creative Journal for Children: A
Guide for Parents, Teachers, and
Counselors,* 27
Creative thinking
in play activity, xi
questions, alibis and mind stretchers
for, 35-39
Creativity
cooking and, 124-127
intelligence and, xi-xii
The Crows of Pearlblossom, 192
Cultural attitudes, 139-142
Cultural diversity, 137-166
artistic creativity and, 146-148
basic needs and, 138-139
body language and, 142-144
game playing and, 157-158
guidelines for appreciating, 152-154
historical aspects of, 153
holidays and, 155-157
language and, 148-150
mythology and, 150-152
pen pals and, 154-155
shortwave radio and, 159
time concepts and, 144-146
"Culturgrams" brochures, 161
Cuttings, plants from, 111-112

D

"Daft Days" (Scottish holidays), 41
*The Days of My Life: A Journal for the
Teen Years,* 27
Death
cemetery tours and, 55-63
cultural attitudes about, 140-141
De Bono, Edward, 42
Déjà vu, 179
*Developing the Creative Edge in
Photography,* 81
de Vries, Peter, 41
Diaries and journals
by children, 15-27
dream analysis with, 19-20, 170-171
by families, 23-25
for gardening, 109-110
guidelines for starting, 17
photographic, 72
reasons for, 16

resources for, 27-29
rules for, 26-27
types of, 17-26
The Diary of a Young Girl, 18, 27
A Dictionary of Days, 41
*Dinner's Ready, Mom: A Cookbook for
Kids,* 133
Divali (Dipawali) (Hindu Festival of
Lights), 155
Divorce, cultural attitudes about, 139
Docks, touring with children, 51
*Doctor Dwarf & Other Poems for
Children,* 194
*A Dog's/Cat's Life: A Journal for You and
Your Pet,* 27
*Doing Children's Museums: A Guide to
225 Hands-On Museums,* 50
Dominoes, 158
Dot-to-dot games, 10
"Double-up Musical Chairs," 86
Dragon, Dragon, and Other Tales, 188
Drawing, from photography, 77-78
Dream analysis, 167-172
Dream journal, 19-20
*Dreams Can Help: A Journal Guide to
Understanding Your Dreams and
Making Them Work For You,* 171
Droodles game, 13
homemade version of, 10

E

EarthBeat! catalog, 161
Eat the Fruit, Plant the Seed, 108, 118
Eat, Think, and Be Healthy!, 133
Educational trips, alternatives for, 49-
54
Emergency fun bag, 6-7
Emigration, experience of, 153
Epitaphs, in cemetery tours, 61-62
Escher, M.C., 34
Esperanto, 149
Estate sales, attending with children, 51
Estimating games, 39
"Ethnic Cultures of America Calendar,"
161
Ethnic events and exhibits, 153
Ethnic foods, 128, 153
cultural diversity and, 138-139
*Everybody's a Winner: A Kid's Guide to
New Sports and Fitness,* 98
*Everybody Wins: 393 Non-Competitive
Games for Young Children,* 98

Exercise, calories and, 131-132
Extrasensory perception (ESP), 181
The Eyes of the Dragon, 193

F

Faces: The Magazine about People, 161
Factory tours, with children, 52
Failure, dealing with, 125
Fairy tales, creating new endings for, 41
Fairy Tales (e.e. cummings), 190
Families
    folklore in, 151-152
    journals by, 24-25
    relationships, revealed in cemetery
        inscriptions, 55-63
*Families: A Celebration of Diversity,
    Commitment, and Love,* 161
Families the World Over series, 161-162
Families Writing, 27-28
Family Book of World Records, 36
The Family Fitness Handbook, 98
Family Pastimes catalog, 98
*Family Words: The Dictionary for People
    Who Don't Know a Frone from a
    Brinkle,* 46-47
*Famous Last Words and Tombstone
    Humor,* 63
*Fantasy and Surreal Postcards: 24 Ready-
    to-Mail Photo-Collages in Full Color,* 47
Farmers' markets, 129
The Fast-Food Guide, 131, 134
Fattypuffs and Thinifers, 195
Faulkner, William, 199
Feelings
    expression of, in diaries, 25-26
    techniques for expressing, 180-181
*50 Simple Things You Can Do to Save the
    Earth,* 54
"Fill-in-the-blanks" games, 40
"Finger pool," 10
Finnegans Wake, 176
Fire department, 52
*A First Dictionary of Cultural Literacy:
    What Our Children Need to Know,* 44
The First Photography Book, 81
"Firsts and Lasts" game, 4
Flatland, 43
Flat Stanley, 47
The Flight of Bembel Rudzuk, 192
Flood myths, 150

Flowers
    edible types of, 113
    gardening with, 103
    Ikebana (Japanese flower arranging),
        117
    legends about, 114
    toxic types of, 109, 113
Folk dancing, 91
Folklore, 148
    in families, 151-152
Food science, 131-132
Foodworks, 134
Foreign films, 147-148
Foreign languages, teaching to children,
    4
Foreign students, activities with, 152
*For Your Own Protection: Stories Science
    Photos Tell,* 81
Fred Hunter's Historical Funeral
    Museum, 63
Friends Around the World game, 162
Frisbee, 90
Fruits
    sculptures from, 114
    tips on growing, 108
Fulghum, Robert, 42-43
The Fun of Cooking, 134
Funeral customs, cultural diversity in,
    140-141
Funny Answers to Foolish Questions, 13

G

Gagline: The Unique Cartoon Caption
    Game, 40, 47
Games
    creative rule changing for, 86-90
    cultural diversity and, 157-158
    designing by children, 96
    new creations, 84-86
*Games of the World: How to Make Them,
    How to Play Them, How They Came to
    Be,* 162
Garage sales, attending with children,
    51
Gardening
    aesthetics of, 113-115
    books about, 113-114
    with children, 101-120
    educational aspects of, 106-110
    Japanese gardening guidelines, 116-
        117
    keeping journals about, 109-110

planning guidelines, 104-105
plant selection tips, 102-103
resources for, 117-120
safety rules for, 106
scientific experiments with, 110-113
See also Flowers; Fruits; Vegetables
Garden of Eden myth, 150
Garfield, Patricia, 169-171
*Gee Wiz! How to Mix Art and Science or
    the Art of Thinking Scientifically,* 47
Geology, cemetery tours and, 60-63
George W. Park Seed Co., 119
"Get Ready, Get Set, GROW!," 118
Give Peace a Chance game, 162
Goblin Market, 195
Godden, Rumer, 199
Good For Me: All About Food in 32 Bites,
    134
The Good Housekeeping Cook Book, 122-
    123
*Graeme Garden's Compendium of Very
    Silly Games,* 41-42
Grave rubbings, 62-63
Great All-Time Excuse Book, 47
Green Thoughts: A Writer in the Garden,
    114, 118
Grocery shopping techniques, 130
Growing media, gardening experiments
    with, 111
Growing Up Amish, 162
Growing Vegetable Soup, 118
Growltiger's Last Stand and Other Poems,
    190
Gudgekin the Thistle Girl, 188
Guiness Book of World Records, 92
Guiness Sports Record Book, 98

H

Haiku poem, 4
Handicapped children, designing
    games for, 96
Hannah Senesh: Her Life and Diary, 28
The Happy Prince and Other Stories, 198
Hawthorne effect, 182-183
HearthSong catalog, 13
Hearts of Wood & Other Timeless Tales,
    194
"Helping Harvest the Land," 157
Herbs and spices, 126
The Hero with a Thousand Faces, 162
Hidden Stories in Plants, 118

"Hide and Squeak," 42
Hirsch, E. D., 44
Historical tours, 52
  of cemeteries, 55-63
The Hobbit, 197
Hobble-de-hoy! The Word Game for Geniuses, 47
Holidays
  cultural diversity and, 155-156
  designing individual, 41
Homemade musical instruments, tips for making, 148
The Hopeful Trout and Other Limericks, 189
Horney, Karen, 18
H-O-R-S-E basketball, 93
Housing, cultural diversity in, 139
"How Do You Feel Today" posters, 180, 184
How to Make a Zero Backwards: An Activity Book for the Imagination, 47
How Tom Beat Captain Najork and His Hired Sportsmen, 191
Hughes, Ted, 199
"Hug tag," 85
Humane society, attending with children, 51
"Human Knot," game, 86
Human Relations Materials (B'nai B'rith Antidefamation League), 162
Hybridization of plants, 112

I

The Igloo, 163
Ikebana (Japanese flower arranging), 117
Ikebana: Spirit and Technique, 118
Illusions, 48
Imagination Towers game, 45-46
In America series, 161-162
Indian kickball, 157
Individualized food portions, 126
Information Center on Children's Cultures, 154-155, 163
Insects, gardening and, 108-109
Intelligence, creativity and, xi-xii
International language, 149
International table manners, 133
In the Beginning: Creation Stories From Around the World, 151, 163
In Two Worlds: A Yup'ik Eskimo Family, 163

"I Packed My Grandmother's Trunk" game, 3
I Spy game, 2
It's All in Your Head: A Guide to Understanding Your Brain and Boosting Your Brain Power, 184
It Was On Fire When I Lay Down On It, 42

J

Japanese gardens, 116-117
"Joseph Campbell and The Power of Myth with Bill Moyers," 150, 163
Junk Food — What It Is, What It Does, 134

K

Kettman, Michael, 92-93
Kickball, 157
Kids Are Natural Cooks: Child-Tested Recipes for Home and School Using Natural Foods, 134
The Kids' Book of Questions, 13
Kids Can Cook, 134
Kids Cooking: A Very Slightly Messy Manual, 134
A Kid's First Book of Gardening, 118
"Kids' Kitchen" video, 134
Kids Meeting Kids Can Make a Difference, 155
Kincher, Jonni, 171
The King of the Hummingbirds, 188
Kitchen Fun, 134
Kitchen safety, 123
Kite flying, 96
Kitsch, activities with, 38
Klauke, Amy, 137
The Klutz Book of Card Games (for Card Sharks and Others), 13
"Know Your Potato" game, 158
Kodak photography booklets, 82
Kohl, Herb, 37
Kumin, Maxin, 199
Kwanzaa festival, 156

L

Labels, learning to read, 131-132
The Land I Lost: Adventures of a Boy in Vietnam, 163
Landsailing boats, 92
Landscaping with children, 108

The Last Legal Spitfire and Other Little-Known Facts About Sports, 98
Leeses Webster, 194
Left-hemisphere dominance in brain, 179-180
Let's Grow! 72 Gardening Adventures with Children, 118
Levine, Robert, 144
Liars' Book of World Records and Astonishing Feats, 44
Libraries, visits to, 51
Lifespans, cultural differences in, 154
Liking Myself: Assertiveness Training for Ages 5–9, 184
Linear time, cultural attitudes toward, 144-145
Linnea's Windowsill Garden, 119
The Lion and the Puppy and Other Stories for Children, 197
Literary Gourmet: Menus from Masterpieces, 135
Literature
  cultural differences in, 148
  See also Books for children
Little Daniel and the Jewish Delicacies, 164
The Little Pigs' First Cookbook, 135
The Little Prince, 199
"London Bridge," cultural variations on, 157-158
Long-term memory, 177
Looking Backward, 43
The Lore of Flowers, 119
Loudmouse, 198
A Louisa May Alcott Diary, 28
"Lucid dreaming," 170
Luilak (Netherlands' holiday), 155
Lukewarm temperature, sensitivity to, 174
Lullabies, 149
Lurie, Alison, 199

M

Mad Libs, 13
  creative revisions of, 10
Magazines
  issues of foreign, 153
  for sports, 94
  See also resource list at end of each chapter
The Magic Door, 191
The Man Who Lived Alone, 191

Maps
  cultural diversity and, 152
  photography and, 73-74
Martha's Best Friend, 196
Martha's New Daddy, 196
Martha's New School, 196
Martial arts, 148
The Marzipan Pig, 192
Mask-making, 148
Math skills
  cemetery tours and, 57-59
  cooking and, 126
Max and the Baby-sitter, 196
Max's Daddy Goes to the Hospital, 196
Max's New Baby, 196
"Maybe Tuesday," 41
Medicine
  plants used in, 109
  transcultural discipline of, 141-142
Memory, 176-179
  games for improving, 2, 177-179
  long-term memory, 177
  sensory register stage, 177
  short-term memory, 177
Metcalf, Peter A., 140-141
"Method of Loci," 177-178
Military bases, visits to, 51
Mnemonics, 179
Mòbius strip, 34
Monopoly (board game), 87
Monument designs, cemetery tours
  and, 61-62
More Science Experiments You Can Eat,
  135
Moslem graphic art, 148
Mostly Michael, 28
The Mouse, the Monster and Me:
  Assertiveness Training for Ages 8–12,
  184
"Muk" (Eskimo game), 158
Multinewspapers company, 153
Museums
  children's, 50
  unusual, 53
Music, cultural differences in, 146-147
My First Camera Book, 82
My First Cook Book, 135
My Friend's Beliefs: A Young Reader's
  Guide to World Religions, 164
My Own Journal: An illustrated notebook,
  28

My Shadow, 196
"Mystery photos," project, 74
Mythology, 150-151

N

Names found in cemeteries, 55-57
National Gardening Association, 119
National Geographic World, 164
Nature walk, 94
Ned Kelly and the City of the Bees, 193
Negative images, photography and, 66
Neighborhood picnics, 95
"Never-seen-before" walk, 94
The New Diary, 28
Newspaper tours, 52
Newton at the Bat: The Science in Sports,
  98-99
New Year's Resolutions game, 3
Nicole Visits an Amish Farm, 164
Nightmare Help: A Guide for Parents and
  Teachers, 171-172
Nightmares
  artistic expression of, 171-172
  incidence of, in children, 168
"No-Connections" game, 3
Nodding, cultural differences about,
  142
Nose-tapping, 142-143
Nutrition, 125, 131-132

O

O'Brien, Margaret, 18
Oddkins: A Fable for All Ages, 194
Offbeat museums and exhibits, 53
Old Possum's Book of Practical Cats, 190
Omni magazine, 34
101 Amusing Ways to Develop Your
  Child's Thinking Skills and Creativity, 48
Only One Woof, 191
On Monday When It Rained, 184
The Open Door: When Writers First
  Learned to Read, 200
"Opposites" game, 3
Optical illusions, 172-173
Oriental dance, 148
Oriental restaurants, 129
Out to Lunch! Jokes About Food, 135
The Ox-Cart Man, 191
Oxymorons, 33-34
  dressing as, 38

P

Paper airplane contests, 10
Paper-and-pencil quickies, 9-10
Parade Magazine, 35
Paradoxes
  examples of, 32-34
  mòbius strip as, 34
Paraskiing, 92
Pasta, cooking guidelines for, 128-129
Pen pals, 154-155
People, 164
People-watching, during waiting
  periods, 2-4
Permanent Californians, 63-64
Permanent New Yorkers, 63-64
Permanent Parisians, 64
Personal feelings diary, 17-19, 25-26,
  93
Peter Rabbit's Cookery Book, 135
Peter Rabbit's Gardening Book, 119
Pets, tips for photographing, 74
"Photo comics," 75
"Photo-fakery," 77
Photography
  book of changes with, 76
  for children, 65-81
  collecting props for, 78
  creative projects with, 77-78
  guidelines and techniques for, 67-71
  projects for children, 71-74
  science safari with, 75
  uses for old photos, 79-80
Physical activity, 83-97
Pileup Game, 184
Ping-pong, 88
Placebo effect, 183
Plant press, 115
Playfair: Everybody's Guide to
  Noncompetitive Play, 84, 99
Poker, 88
Police department, visits to, 52
Poor Little Stephen Girard, 198
Positive thinking
  athletic performance and, 93
  techniques for, 181-182
Privacy, cultural attitudes about, 141-
  142
The Private and Personal Reading Journal
  of..., 28
Problem solving games, 42-43
Propagating plants, 112

Proverbs, new endings for, 40-41
Psychic abilities, 181
Psychological dynamics, 181
Psychologist, visiting with children, 181
Psychology for children, 167-185
    dream analysis, 167-172
    experiments for, 179-183
    memory testing, 176-179
    physiological aspects, 172-176
    special effects, 182-183
Psychology for Kids: 40 Fun Tests that Help You Learn About Yourself, 184-185
Publishers, selected list of, 201-203
"Puddle walk," 94-95
Pygmalion effect, 183

Q
"Quiche, Ratatouille, Avocado, Muesli" game, 42

R
Radio studios, 52
Reaction times, tests for, 174-175
Real estate records, 51
Recipes developed by children, 125
Recycling activities, 53-54
Religious beliefs
    cemetery tours and, 59-60
    creation myths, 163
    cultural diversity in, 164
Relaxation techniques, 175-176
Rembrandt Takes a Walk, 196-197
Report cards on parents, 9-10
Restaurants
    ethnic diversity and, 138-139
    tours of, 127
"Reverse Score" game, 86
Ringer catalog, 119
Rites of passage, cultural attitudes about, 140
Roethke, Theodore, 199
Roosevelt, Theodore, 18
Rootabaga Stories, 195
Rorschach test, 180
Rose gardening, with thornless roses, 106-107
Rosenthal effect, 183

S
Safety
    cooking with children and, 123
    for gardening, 106
Salad bars, 126
Sand gardens, 116
Sand, George, 199
Sarton, May, 199
Savant, Marilyn vos, 35
Scarecrows, tips for making, 108
School's Out — Now What? Creative Choices for Your Child, 54
Science
    food and, 131-132
    gardening and, 110-113
    sports and, 95-97
Science Experiments You Can Eat, 135
Science safari, 75
Scrabble (board game), 87
Scrapbook journal, 21
Seasonal foods, 130
The Second Centering Book, 183
Seeds from edible fruits, gardening with, 108
Self-esteem techniques, photography and, 65-66
"Self-fulfilling prophecy," 183
Self-motivated science projects, 113
Self-reference paradoxes, 33
Senses, psychological aspects of, 172-176
"Sensory register," 177
"Shalom Sesame," 164
Sharing the Joy of Nature: Nature Activities for All Ages, 99
"Sharing Through Music: A Multicultural Experience," 164
Shelters: From Tepee to Igloo, 165
Shevoroshkin, Vitaly (Dr.), 150
The Shooting of Dan McGrew, 196
Short-term memory, 177
Shortwave Goes to School — A Teacher's Guide to Using Shortwave Radio in the Classroom, 159
Shortwave radio, 159
Silly games, inventions for, 41-42
Single-lens reflex (SLR) camera, 67
Sinister Garden (San Diego, California), 109
Ski-Driving, 92
Skijaks, 91

Skin sensitivity, 173-174
Skipping Stones: A Multi-ethnic Children's Forum, 137-138, 165
The Slightly Irregular Fire Engine, 189
Small World Celebrations, 165
Smell, sense of, 174
Smith & Hawken catalog, 119
Smith of Wootton Major, 197
Snack foods, children's projects with, 126
Snakes in myths, 150-151
Sniglets game, 4, 13
Snow boarding, 92
Snow-White and the Seven Dwarfs, 193
Soccer (football), 157
Social Studies School Service materials, 165
Social values, language and, 149-150
Soil preparation tips for gardening, 104
Soil-testing projects, 112
Solitaire, 88
Somehow Tenderness Survives: Stories of Southern Africa, 165
Song of Sedna, 165
Sorry! (board game), 87
So You Bought a Shortwave Radio! A Get Acquainted Guide to the Wide World of Shortwave, 159
Spark, Muriel, 199
Specialty food outlets, 129
Spectacles, 189
Spontaneity, creativity and, xii
Sports
    performance records, 93
    unusual types of, 91-93
SportScience, 95, 99
Sports Illustrated for Kids, 99
Sports science, 95-97
Sportworks, 99
Stafford, Jean, 200
Stanley Foundation, 37
Stationary bicycles, 93
Stick Up For Yourself! Every Kid's Guide to Personal Power and Positive Self-Esteem, 180, 185
Stories for Children, 196
Story Number 3, 192
The Story-Teller, 195
Stuart Little, 199
Student Letter Exchange, 154
Stunt games, 39

Stunt kits, 96

Sunflowers, 119

Sungrams, 66

Super Flyers, 99

Supposes, 48

Swan Lake, 191

Swenson, May, 200

Symbols common to many cultures, 151

Symmetry in photography, 74

T

Table manners, 132-133

T.A. for Kids and Grown-Ups Too: How to Feel OK About Yourself and Other People, 185

T.A. for Teens, 185

T.A. for Tots, 185

Team sports, 89

Technology, sports and, 97

Television studio, 52

Tell Me About Yourself: How to Interview Anyone from Your Friends to Famous People, 28

The Temptation of Wilfred Malachey, 189

Tennis, 88-89

"Ten Ways Not to..." creative thinking game, 37

Tet (Vietnamese New Year), 157

Then and Now: A Book of Days, 28

The Three Astronauts, 190

They Have A Word For It: A Lighthearted Lexicon of Untranslatable Words and Phrases, 149, 165

The 13 Clocks, 197

"Thrips," 42

Thrump-O-Moto, 190

Tic-tac-toe, 5, 158

Tiger Lilies and Other Beastly Plants, 119

Time, cultural attitudes towards, 144-145

Time capsules, 21-22

Time travel, paradoxes and, 33

To Hell With Dying, 198

Tongue, sensitivity of, 174

Tongue twisters, 8-9

Topiary gardens, 115

Tortillitas Para Mama and Other Nursery Rhymes in Spanish and English, 166

Transcultural medicine, 141-142

Travel guides by children, 38

The Travelers' Guide to Asian Customs and Manners, 166

Traveling

  alternative destinations for, 49-54

  games for, 6-9

Trick Photography: Crazy Things You Can Do With Cameras, 82

Trouble in Bugland: A Collection of Inspector Mantis Mysteries, 194

Tug-of-war, 158

The Tunnel of Love, 41

"Two Kinds of People" game, 37

"Type T" personality, 175-176

U

Underfoot: An Everyday Guide to Exploring the American Past, 64

The Unanswered Question: Six Talks at Harvard, 147

UNICEF, U.S. Committee for, 163, 166

  holiday calendar, 155

  trick-or-treating project, 153-154

Universal Esperanto Association, 149

Unusual Airplanes, 48

V

Vases for flowers, 114-115

Vegetables

  gardening guidelines for, 102-103

  sculptures from, 114

Venus fly-trap, 112

"Via Air Mail: Your Guide to Overseas Penpals," 155

Vicious Circles and Infinity: An Anthology of Paradoxes, 48

The Victory Garden Kids' Book: A Beginner's Guide to Growing Vegetables, Fruits, and Flowers, 119

Video cameras, activities with, 80-81

Video games, activities with, 80-81, 90

"Video Letter from Japan," 166

A Visit from Dr. Katz, 194

Visual paradoxes, 34

Vocabulary development, cooking and, 125

Volleyball, changing rules in, 89

Voltaire, 200

W

Waiting games, 1-6

Walking with children, 94-95

Wallechinsky, David, 44

Wallyball, 92

Warm and Cold, 194-195

Water balloons, 90

Wayside Gardens catalog, 120

Weightlessness, exercise and, 96-97

"What if" game, 12

"What's the Question?," 5

"What's wrong" walk, 94

"What's Wrong with this Picture" game, 39

Where in the World game, 162

White Flower Farms catalog, 120

White Stone Day, 41

White-water ballooning, 92

"Who lives here" walk, 95

"Why Not?" list, 9

The Widow and the Parrot, 199

Wiseman, Anne Sayre, 171-172

Wish Lists, 9

Wish You Were Here, 198

Women's Bodies, Women's Dreams, 169

"World Calendar," 161

The World is Round, 196

The World's Best Sports Riddles & Jokes, 99

World's Toughest Tongue Twisters, 13

World Wide Games catalog, 99

Writer's Journal, 22-23

Writing Down the Days: 365 Creative Journaling Ideas for Young People, 29

Writing for Kids, 29

Y

You Come Too: Favorite Poems for Young Readers, 191

Your Child's Dreams, 169

Youth, cultural attitudes about, 140